LEGAL NOTICE:

TABLE *of* CONTENTS

FOREWORD *by* CHRIS YOUNG

Cofounder of ChefSteps, Coauthor of Modernist Cuisine: The Art and Science of Cooking

At ChefSteps, we've always relied on a community of curious cooks who work together to raise questions and solve problems collaboratively. Grace has been part of the ChefSteps community from the very beginning, and is always enthusiastic about our commitment to building an online community around cooking.

So when Grace came to us for Kickstarter support earlier this year, it only made sense that we'd consider supporting her and her partner Xi in their endeavor. Not simply because they had supported us, but because the very nature of their Kickstarter was aligned with ChefSteps' vision: They wanted to build something that would make cooking better, easier, and more approachable, and they wanted to do it by asking like-minded people to directly contribute to their vision.

But we still had to ask: In an already-saturated market, why another sous vide device? The answer was as simple as Codlo itself. Unlike its ever-cheaper competitors, this device is design-forward, user-friendly, and approachable to cooks at all skill levels. The goal, also aligned with ChefSteps' own ethos, was to give enthusiastic cooks the ability to cook more creatively; to bring the convenience and consistency of sous vide into every kitchen.

Though we haven't gotten our own Codlo yet, we can't wait to start experimenting when we do. We wish Grace and Xi the very best of luck, and we're proud to continue to support communities of cooks who collaborate and think creatively about how to cook smarter.

Chris Young
Cofounder of ChefSteps,
Coauthor of Modernist Cuisine: The Art and
Science of Cooking

PREFACE *by* GRACE

This book contains all my notes, learnings and recipes on sous-vide cooking that I wanted to share with you since my discovery of this technique years ago. It's all you ever need to learn and master the foundations of sous-vide cooking, in a fraction of the time I took.

You'll grasp the key techniques, build a solid food knowledge base and constantly impress with your cooking. For those who are new to sous-vide cooking, I'd suggest reading the Introduction and Tips sections before trying out the recipes.

My cooking philosophy is to be practical yet impressive, and that's reflected in my recipes. Minimal fuss with maximum impact. Recipes are organized by ingredients, and within each ingredient section, by increasing complexity. So just like a course, it's best to try the recipes (within each ingredient section) in order. But feel free to start with your favorite ingredient section!

In the beginning, you may find the need to constantly refer to the Technique and Safety sections. This will reduce over time as you go through the book, trying out each recipe. Sous-vide needs a bit of practice, but once you get going you'll never turn back!

Sous-vide has fundamentally changed the way I cook and eat at home, I hope it'll become an indispensable cooking technique for you too.

If you'd told me more than a year ago that I would be writing a sous-vide book, and at the same time quit my job to jump into designing and manufacturing Codlo today - I would have

told you to dial down the crazy. But life is always unpredictable and full of surprises, isn't it?

Working on Codlo felt like tasting sous-vide chicken breast for the first time - mindblowing. I never could have imagined that "work" could be so much more engaging and fulfilling. That's what passion leads to, as I'm incredibly excited to share what I've discovered and learned about sous-vide

cuisine with you - professional chefs have had too much fun with this for a while now!

You have made Codlo and this Sous-Vide Guide possible. Without your raving support throughout since our humble beginnings, all of these would never have happened. You'll always be our heroes and thank you for your support to make Codlo a reality.

I have my co-founder Xi to thank too, as I couldn't have done it without his impeccable eye for design, engineering expertise, photography skills and constant encouragement which kept me going.

Finally, I'd like to thank Scott, Anne, Johan and the Chefsteps community for their comments on the initial draft, it made this book even more epic.

Enjoy the journey of discovering sous-vide cooking as you go through this Guide. Happy cooking!

Grace

Working on Codlo felt like tasting sous-vide chicken breast for the first time - mindblowing.

INTRODUCTION *to* SOUS-VIDE

WHAT IS SOUS-VIDE COOKING ABOUT?

Sous-vide (pronounced "sue-veed") is a cooking technique that uses low and precise temperatures to create amazing dishes. Ingredients are usually sealed in an airtight, food-safe plastic bag and gently cooked for a minimum amount of time in a temperature-controlled pot of water (chefs often call this a "water bath").

Originally used as an industrial food preservation method, sous-vide was then adopted by a prominent Michelin 3-star restaurant in France to cook foie gras in the 1970s. It turns out that foie gras cooked at a lower, precise temperature retained its appearance better, had a nicer texture and didn't lose an excessive amount of moisture either! That's not surprising - after all, the key to great cooking is temperature control.

Given the higher temperatures used, most conventional cooking methods require our constant attention to avoid overcooking food. Sous-vide is the exact opposite: instead of focusing on only timing, sous-vide is all about cooking ingredients gently at their ideal, lower temperatures until they reach that core temperature throughout. Perfection.

Sous-vide frees up your time, yields perfectly cooked results without overcooking. Sous-vide food is juicy, moist and evenly cooked throughout to your preference. It's foolproof, stress-free and healthy cooking at it's best.

Cooking sous-vide is easy (especially with Codlo!): All you need to do is set your preferred cooking time and temperature, seal food items in a bag so that it's airtight and submerge it in a temperature-controlled water bath to cook for a minimum period of time. You only attend to it once it's done!

"Sous-vide frees up your time, yields perfectly cooked results without overcooking...it's foolproof, stress-free and healthy cooking at it's best."

WHY IS SOUS-VIDE *Awesome*?

We find that sous-vide can sometimes be quite tricky to explain in words. Hence, here are a couple of pictures as a quick summary why we think it's amazing!

With sous-vide cooking, you'll have:

1) Complete control of the texture and desired finish of food.

How do you like your egg yolk? Here's a gooey, honey-like one at 63°C (145.4°F) for our Spaghetti Carbonara.

2) Juicy, tender and nutritious food. Yes, even chicken breast can be tasty!

Grilled chicken breast - dry, fibrous and chewy.

Sous-vide chicken breast - juicy, moist and tender.

3) Food evenly cooked throughout without the "gradient-of-doneness."

Grilled steak, with a "gradient of doneness"

Overcooked

Undercooked "rare"

Perfect "Medium"

Sous-vide steak, perfectly medium throughout

4) Re-experience new tastes and textures of familiar dishes.

| Raw salmon sashimi | Buttery sous-vide salmon, best of both worlds | Classic grilled, flaky salmon |

Experience mind-blowing new tastes and textures with sous-vide cooking!

OTHER BENEFITS *of* COOKING SOUS-VIDE

WHAT IS SOUS-VIDE COOKING ABOUT?

Since we started cooking sous-vide, we noticed other great upsides to this cooking technique too. Living on a healthier (and tastier) lifestyle while saving money & time - sous-vide is a clear win-win.

IMPROVED HEALTH & LIFESTYLE

Reduced usage of oil
Fresh ingredients are cooked in their own juices with sous-vide. Adding fat or oil is optional in most cases.

Even the classic, indulgent French duck confit, whereby duck legs are cooked slowly completely immersed in its own fat, can be done using sous-vide just with 1 tablespoon of fat. This is because the airtight condition in sous-vide cooking ensures the 1 tablespoon of (melted) fat completely encases the meat at all times throughout the cooking process.

Reduced need for fattier cuts of meat
In traditional cooking methods, fat and sauces are used as replacements for the natural juiciness lost when food items are cooked beyond their optimum temperature.

With sous-vide, fattier cuts become unnecessary since the meat retains its nutrients and natural moisture. In fact, fattier cuts are best avoided as the fat doesn't render with low temperature cooking.

Consumption of fats (especially saturated fats) are reduced to a minimum, with no detrimental impact on taste, texture and flavor. Woohoo!

Beef Short Ribs

Low and slow cooking tenderises tougher cuts of meat.

All you need is a quick sear on a hot pan prior to serving.

SAVES MONEY

Sous-vide is excellent with cheaper and tougher cuts of meat. The low and slow cooking treatment transforms such cuts into tender and tasty masterpieces, without even looking (literally). Beef short ribs, pork cheeks and lamb shanks are notable examples and restaurant favorites. The pictures above show beef short ribs that I use in one of my recipes (Short Ribs Tagliata, page 80).

SAVES TIME

More importantly, you'll have more time in your day despite cooking more often! Sous-vide cooking is multi-tasking taken to a new level.

With a little planning, you could host small dinner parties with significantly less stress. Things can be prepared in advanced and finished last minute on the stove/oven/grill, with fantastic results.

WHAT'S DIFFERENT *About* SOUS-VIDE COOKING?

WHAT SHOULD WE EXPECT?

Emphasis on time and temperature

- **A different yet complimentary cooking technique**. Sous-vide is a form of low and slow cooking that cooks food at a lower, ideal temperature for a longer period of time until it's just right.

- **Larger margin of error for time**. Food will not be overcooked if left in the water bath for longer than the minimum cooking time, as they are held at their lower, ideal temperatures anyway – which is why sous-vide is great for dinner parties!

- **Time and temperature is key**: this varies according to ingredient type, thickness, food safety considerations and desired finish (i.e. "doneness"). Don't worry, I'll guide you through our carefully designed charts and recipes in the next section.

- **Some advance preparation and planning needed**. Especially if you want go ultra-low and slow, such as cooking a big roast for 72 hours. The good news? Most of the cooking is done unattended.

- **Food safety is crucial**. Food should be cooked for at least the minimum length of time advised in the recipe for safety. Refer to the Food Safety section for more information.

Better taste, consistent results

- **Even texture from edge-to-edge**. For example, your steak can now be cooked perfectly medium throughout, without the "gradient-of-doneness" of overcooked exterior to undercooked core.

- **A finishing step**. Sous-vide cooked meat generally benefits from a quick sear in the pan as a final step, to give it a nice crust. The next page tells you more on the usual sous-vide cooking process.

- **Sous-vide cooking concentrates flavors** since food items are cooked intensely in their own juices. You'll need fewer spices, herbs, fat and flavoring for the same effect through sous-vide cooking.

- **Serve on warmed plates, immediately**. Given the lower cooking temperatures, sous-vide meals get colder faster than the norm. Serve it fresh!

- **Sous-vide is awesome for most ingredients**. Sous-vide is great for meat, delicate seafood, root vegetables, eggs, custards and fruits. Green vegetables (e.g. broccoli, green beans) however may not see much benefit from the sous-vide technique. See Sous-Vide Tips section for more details.

SOUS-VIDE IN 5 STEPS:

1. PREHEAT
Preheat the water bath in your sous-vide setup to target temperature.

2. PREPARE
Just like other cooking methods, do your initial food preparation such as chopping, deboning, seasoning, marinating, brining etc.

3. SEAL
This step usually involves placing ingredients in food-grade plastic bags in a single, non-overlapping layer and making them airtight. There are 2 ways to do this: using a vacuum sealer or the water displacement method. Please refer to Technique and Equipment section for more details.

4. COOK
Once the water bath reaches target temperature, fully submerge the sealed bags in it to cook for a minimum amount of time. The time and temperature combinations will largely depend on the type of ingredient, its thickness, your personal preference and food safety considerations.

5. FINISH
Once food is cooked, the final step usually involves a quick searing process to give it a traditional outer texture prior to serving. If saving for later use, you can also quickly chill the cooked food for refrigeration.

SOUS-VIDE *Tips*

GET THE MOST FROM YOUR COOKING

General

- **Braised = awesome sous-vide**. Almost anything that can be braised benefits from being cooked sous-vide.
- **Beans, grains and pasta**: If you're cooking these sous-vide, make sure you leave enough expansion room in the bag.
- **Cooking times depend on thickness and tenderness** of the food. It can range from as little as 20-30 minutes (lean fish, foie gras) to as long as 72 hours (spare ribs, tougher cuts of meat). Please refer to the Recipes section for temperature charts by ingredient as a starting point.
  - * **Food thickness** (rather than weight) determines how long it'll take for it to reach target temperature throughout. Cooking time increases exponentially with thickness.
  - * **Tender cuts** generally have shorter cooking times (1-2 hours depending on thickness). Holding them for longer than 3 hours may create a mushy texture, as it gets too tender.
  - * **Tougher cuts** (leaner or muscular sections) are brought up to temperature based on the thickness of the portion, but also benefit from additional slow cooking time to become more tender, just like braising. Depending on preference, some cuts can be cooked up to 48-72 hours.

Seasoning

- **Sous-vide intensifies flavors**. Therefore, you'd use only about 1/2 of the herbs, spices and aromatics usually required. It's always better to season less (if at all) when cooking, as you can always adjust seasonings after it's cooked in your finishing step.
- **It's best to season meat after cooking** (except brining) for maximum flexibility to cook-chill and reheat later. See Food Safety section for details on cook-chill.
- **Avoid using olive oil to cook for a long time** (more than 1 hour) at a low temperature as it tends to produce a metallic aftertaste. Use butter, canola or sunflower oil instead.
- **Use fresh, raw garlic sparingly** as the smell and flavor intensifies when cooked sous-vide for a long time. A better bet would be a tiny pinch of garlic powder.
- **If brining meat** prior to cooking it sous-vide, make sure it's rinsed well beforehand

to avoid it being too salty. Please refer to the Techniques section for more information on brining.

- **Alcohol should be cooked off** before adding it to a pouch and sealing, as it'll produce vapor and lead to uneven cooking.

Cooking

- **Don't overstuff the water bath** with pouches, you need some space for water circulation and even cooking.
- **Keep meat cuts fairly thin** to reduce cooking times. Minimum cooking times increase exponentially with thickness. You can easily do this by slicing them into portion-sized servings before cooking.
- **For thicker cuts of meat** (1.5 inches and above), stick to the suggested cooking time and temperature for food safety. We recommend pre-searing the surface of the thick piece of meat prior to the sous-vide process to reduce surface bacteria. This also improves the flavor development of the meat over the long cooking time. There is an exception to this: pre-searing lamb tends to intensify the strong smell, hence is not recommended.
- **Sealed pouches tend to float a little** when cooking at higher temperatures (above 70°C / 158°F) or when fattier cuts are used. This is normal and occurs due to water vapor pressure in the bag. It's still safe to consume, but you should place something (e.g. a plate) to weigh it down to stay submerged for even, safe cooking.
- **Permeating smells or a slightly 'murky' water** bath can occur, especially when cooking at a higher temperature, even though sous-vide cooking is done in a pouch. This is normal as sous-vide bags are not perfectly airtight.
- **Holding food at cooking temperature for too long** will result in an overly tender and mushy texture. A good rule of thumb is not to hold food for longer than twice the minimum cooking time. If you need to pasteurize food, additional holding is needed (see each food section's Codlo Guide page).

What should not be cooked sous-vide?

- **Whole birds in one piece**. Dark and white meats have different (optimal) cooking times and temperatures. Vacuum sealing them whole is also tricky due to the cavity. It's best to break down the parts to cook dark and white meat separately.
- **Green vegetables** are best eaten raw, or after a quick sautéing or blanching.
- **Ground meat** should be handled with care given the higher surface area for bacterial growth. Pre-searing the surface or cooking at a higher temperature for an extended time would help.

What is CODLO?

Upgrade your cooker into a sous-vide machine

Make the most of your existing kitchen technology. Codlo pairs up with your existing cooker and transforms it into a lean mean sous-vide machine.

And it's really easy to set up - you can do it in seconds.

Precise temperature control

We faced a significant challenge when creating the brains and software for Codlo. How could we precisely control the temperature of any cooker on the planet?

With our Fluid algorithm, Codlo learns and adapts to your individual cooker from first use, achieving temperature regulation of ±0.2°C / ±0.4 °F. Clever little thing.

Compact & takes up no space

We designed Codlo to look and feel as incredible as the powerful technology we built into it. The result is a unibody design that fits on your palm.

Codlo requires no space at all - it plugs straight into your kitchen's wall socket and stays there. Zero kitchen counter space needed.

Safe and energy-efficient

With Codlo, there is minimal water evaporation and no exposed heating coils.Codlo's unibody design ensures all electrical circuits are kept far away from potential water spills. Its temperature probe and cord is fully sheathed in 100% food grade high-temperature polymer.

Codlo saves up to 50% of energy used in cooking, because heat generated goes to cooking your food, not lost as residual heat.

3 Simple Steps TO USING CODLO

PLUG IN CODLO AND YOUR COOKER

- Plug in Codlo into your kitchen wall outlet and plug your cooker's power plug into Codlo's base

- Turn on Codlo and your cooker (start your engines!)

INSERT THE TEMPERATURE SENSOR

- Unwind Codlo's temperature sensor and place it in the cooker (which you should fill with water)

- You can place your cooker's lid over the cord - it'll be fine

SET TEMPERATURE (AND TIME)

- Just like an oven, set your temperature, and time if you need it

- You can find perfect cooking temperature for most foods throughout this Guide

- You're now ready to cook sous-vide!

HOW TO GET *Your Very Own Codlo*

PREORDER AT CODLO.COM

We've had a successful Kickstarter campaign and are in the process of bringing Codlo to production. You can see our latest progress updates at **codlo.com/blog**.

You can still get in on the action at **codlo.com**. Pre-order your Codlo now at our special pre-retail price to reserve yours in line!

WILL CODLO SUIT ME?

Codlo works with any analogue water-heating appliance. Slow cookers and rice cookers work best, but food warmers, tabletop roasters or even a coffee urn can work too!

Codlo will be shipped globally, and comes in 4 plug types:

US (110V-120V)   EU Schuko (220V-240V)   UK (220V-240V)   AU/NZ (220V-240V)

RECIPES: *Introduction*

I bet you're hopping with excitement to cook some amazing dishes right now! Do spare a minute to read this section beforehand, as it'll save you time when trying out these recipes afterwards.

The recipes are organized by ingredients - feel free to jump around and try out your favorite ingredients first. Within each section, recipes are ordered by increasing complexity - I do recommend that you start with the simpler ones!

Each section is packed with useful tips gathered throughout the years of cooking sous-vide at home, plus a temperature chart as reference.

Key things to note:
1. All recipes in this book assume food items are cooked from refrigerated temperature. If you're cooking or reheating from frozen, do refer to the Food Safety section on the additional cooking time required.
2. If applicable, each recipe comes with various options for time and temperature combinations to achieve a certain desired "finish," as well as pasteurization if preferred (labeled with the 🌟 symbol).
3. Cup measurements follow US standards.
4. Thickness of food (especially meat) is important in sous-vide. Please pay attention to this and cook food for the recommended minimum cooking time. Time and thickness guidelines are provided in temperature charts to indicate appropriate cooking times.
5. Preheating time estimates are based on a 500W rice cooker. This may vary depending on the type and size of your cooker. Please adjust your preparation time accordingly.

RECIPES: *Table* OF CONTENTS

EGGS

Eggs are the perfect ingredient to start with in sous-vide cooking. There's a reason why people go ga-ga over them! The results are fun, easy and impressive, plus you don't even need a bag to cook them in - they come in their own protective shells! Just gently plop them in the water bath with a spoon and cook at the target temperature for a set amount of time. Once done, serve them straight from the shell onto the plate.

Eggs are very temperature-sensitive. Its texture can change drastically within the 60°C - 65°C (140°F - 149°F) range. Egg white starts coagulating at 60°C (140°F) and completely sets around 80°C (176°F); whereas egg yolk starts coagulating at 65°C (149°F) and sets at 70°C (158°F).

With that knowledge, you can construct your perfect egg by choosing the consistency of yolk and white that you like - check out the Egg Temperature Chart in the next page. The 63°C (145.4°F) egg is a popular favorite for poached egg substitute, because you'll get custardy yolk that is so good and creamy that you'll want to mop it up with anything on your plate!

> The 63°C (145.4°F) egg is a popular favorite ... custardy yolk that is so good and creamy that you'll want to mop it up with anything on your plate!

CODLO'S SOUS-VIDE GUIDE TO *Your* PERFECT EGG

Sous-vide turns the humble egg into creamy, indulgent globules of desire. Here's how you achieve any kind of egg consistency you like!

THE EGG YOLK SPECTRUM

>>> *Increasing* THICKNESS >>>

Flowing "Cream"	*Viscous "Honey"*	*Thick "Mayonnaise"*	*Pliable "Camembert"*
61.5 °C / 143.0 °F	63.0 °C / 145.5 °F	64.0 °C / 148.0 °F	68.0 °C / 154.4 °F
60 mins	60 mins	60 mins	60 mins

Perfect for...

SAUCES
Fully cooked to delicate runniness. Perfect for egg-based sauces, spaghetti carbonara or the exotic Asian 'half-boiled egg'.

SOFT BOILED EGGS
The perfect soft-boiled egg. Custardy whites and a thick, honey-like yolk – never settle for less at breakfast!

POACHED EGGS
The egg white and yolk are at the same luscious consistency, creating a perfectly poached egg that smoothly slides out of its shell.

HARD BOILED EGGS
The yolk forms a rich, golden truffle. Firming the whites (see below) creates a tender, melt-in-your-mouth hard-boiled egg.

OPTIONAL: FIRMING THE WHITES

After sous-vide cooking, egg whites are lightly set at a custardy texture.
To bring the whites to a firm, peelable solid without affecting the yolks:

Cool
Your eggs – running tap water is perfect

▶ **Boil**
Your eggs at 100°C for 4 minutes

▶ **Cool**
Your eggs again to yummy perfection

BROWN OR WHITE?
White hens produce white eggs, brown/red hens produce brown eggs. There's no difference between the two, but for some reason people generally prefer brown eggs.

FRANKEN EGGS
You can have eggs within eggs, and even multiple-yolked eggs. The largest number of yolks recorded in an egg was 9!

NOTES:
Temperature works for duck and quail eggs too, just halve the time for quail eggs. To pasteurize, cook eggs for 1 hour 15 minutes.

Temperature   Timing

SLOW COOKED EGG WITH *Caviar* & ASPARAGUS

The humble egg is an extremely versatile ingredient. This simple recipe is ridiculously easy, looks great and the sous-vide cooked egg will make it out of this world!

Ingredients:

- 4 free range eggs
- 175g (6 oz) asparagus spears, trimmed and washed
- Salt and black pepper
- 5g (1 tsp) black caviar

Like this one?
Let us know via Twitter @codlo!

Method:

1 hour 15 minutes before
- Set Codlo to preheat water bath to 63.5°C (146°F) with 1 hour cooking time.
- Once target temperature is reached, use a spoon to gently place the eggs in the water bath to cook.

5 minutes before
- Warm the plates in preparation for plating.
- Blanch the asparagus for 2-3 minutes, depending on thickness. Shock them in ice cold water, drain and divide equally among serving plates.

To plate
- Carefully crack the egg on top of the bed of asparagus. Season with salt and black pepper, to taste.
- Finally, add 2.5g (1/2 teaspoon) of caviar on top of the egg and serve immediately.

CHEF'S TIP:
Instead of caviar, you could serve the eggs with homemade hollandaise sauce and a crusty toast (to mop up the lovely sauce!).

EGGS *Benedict* & EGGS ROYALE

I remember the absolute delight and excitement when I first discovered sous-vide - I had eggs for breakfast 2 weeks in a row! You have absolute control over how you'd like your eggs to be, just by varying the temperature. Oh, and the astounded expressions you get when a ready-poached egg is cracked right from its shell onto a toast - priceless.

With sous-vide eggs, the perfect Sunday brunch couldn't be easier. I've also added an easy Hollandaise recipe inspired by Harold McGee, using just a saucepan, whisk and 5 minutes of your time.

Ingredients:

Eggs & Muffin
- 2 free range eggs
- 1 English muffin

Hollandaise Sauce
- 1 large egg yolk
- 8ml (1/2 tbsp) warm water
- 60g (2 oz) cold unsalted butter
- 8ml (1/2 tbsp) lemon juice
- Salt and black pepper

Accompaniments
- 2 slices of Parma ham
- 35g (1.2oz) of smoked salmon

To Finish
- Sprinkle of paprika
- Freshly ground black pepper

Method:

1 hour before
- Set Codlo to preheat water bath to 64°C (147°F) with 1 hour cooking time. Once target temperature is reached, use a spoon to gently place the eggs in the water bath to cook.

5 minutes before
- Slice the English muffin into half and lightly toast them in the oven.
- To make Hollandaise sauce: place the egg yolk, water and butter in a saucepan over low heat, stir gently with a whisk. Once the butter has melted, increase heat slightly to medium-low and whisk vigorously until it thickens. Remove from heat once sauce thickens. Stir in lemon juice. Season with salt and black pepper to taste.

TIP: You can also use white wine vinegar instead of lemon juice.

To plate
- Place toasted halves of the muffin on a plate, topped with Parma ham and smoked salmon respectively. Carefully crack each egg gently on top of the ham and salmon. Drizzle a spoonful of Hollandaise sauce on top of each egg, along with some black pepper and paprika. Serve immediately.

⬮ CHEF'S TIP:

Temperature control is key to avoid curdling the hollandaise sauce. If in doubt, it's better to go lower and slower first as all it takes is a little too much heat for the sauce to curdle.

SPAGHETTI ALLA *Carbonara*

have a friend who is extremely proud of his version of Carbonara. Every time I'm having dinner at his place, I know he'll be breaking out the pancetta and cream.

However Italians seldom use cream in their variations. For my recipe I chose to go with the original - using egg yolks. The perfectly formed egg yolk crown is this dish's pièce de résistance and the volcanic explosion of yolk magma is just fun to watch. It is little things like this that makes me savor life (and food) a little more.

Ingredients:

Egg Topping
- 2 free range eggs

Spaghetti & Sauce
- 2 free range eggs
- 180g (6 oz) spaghetti
- Salt & black pepper
- 30g (1 oz) pecorino cheese, finely grated
- 30g (1 oz) Parmesan, finely grated

To Finish
- 50g (1.7 oz) Parma ham
- Dried thyme

Need some guidance?
Let us know on Twitter via @codlo!

Method:

2 hours 15 minutes before
- Set Codlo to preheat water bath to 61.5°C (143°F) with 1 hour cooking time. Once target temperature is reached, use a spoon to gently place the eggs in the water bath to cook. This will be used for the sauce.

1 hour before
- Repeat the same steps above with the other 2 eggs at 63°C (145°F). Set aside.

TIP: With 63°C (145°F) eggs, you'll get thicker, viscous yolks that bursts and slowly glides down the tower of spaghetti when pierced with a fork. Eggasmic!

15 minutes before
- Bring a large pot of salted water to boil. Cook the spaghetti according to package instructions until al dente.
- Whisk the two 61.5°C (143°F) eggs in a bowl and season with salt and pepper. Add in most of the pecorino cheese and Parmesan. Finally, add the cooked spaghetti to the mixture and toss to coat evenly.
- Warm the plates in preparation for plating.
- Crack and place a 63°C (145°F) egg in a ladle and roll it under running water to gently shave off the egg white, leaving the yolk. Repeat for the other egg and set aside.

To plate
- Use a long-pronged fork to twist the pasta into a nest in the center of a warm plate. Carefully place an egg yolk on top of the pasta nest with some parma ham strands on the side. Finish with a sprinkle of thyme and some remaining cheese.

○ CHEF'S TIP:

61.5°C (143°F) eggs have liquid yolks and lightly set egg whites. Using this instead of the usual raw eggs for your sauce will guarantee results!

POULTRY

C hicken, turkey and duck are amazing when cooked sous-vide. It's popular, available all year round and breast meat is super juicy cooked this way - we can hardly wait to hear what you think once you try it out!

All you need to know are the differences in optimal temperatures for white vs. dark meat. With the exception of duck, chicken and turkey breast meat are considered white whereas the rest (wings, thighs, drumsticks) are dark meat. In general, dark meat has higher optimal temperatures than white meat. Due to these differences, it's best to break down the parts (i.e. not cook a whole bird in one piece) for sous-vide cooking. Please refer to the Poultry Temperature Chart on the next page for guidance.

We recommend going boneless for breast as it's easier to serve right away, or portioned into slices.

For duck breast, the optimal temperature ranges from 57°C (135°F) for medium rare to 70°C (158°F) for well done depending on your preference. The temperature charts in the next page reflect our recommended "doneness".

A final tip on getting duck skin crispy (especially for breasts): as the skin is quite thick, pan fry it over medium heat for 5-6 minutes until golden. Be careful with adding sweet sauces or marinades to the skin as it'll caramelize and burn the skin before it gets nice and crispy.

CODLO'S SOUS-VIDE *Guide* TO POULTRY

CHICKENS AND TURKEYS AND DUCKS, OH MY

THE WING

The wing has 3 segments: the drummette, the middle 'flat' segment containing 2 bones and the tip. Wings are often served as a light meal or bar food, including the Buffalo Wing, invented in 1964. Wings are generally not cooked sous-vide – try barbequing.

THE BREAST

The leanest cut, high in protein. Chicken and turkey are considered white meat, but duck breast is dark. Traditional cooking methods yield relatively tough results, but this is where sous-vide shines!

	Thickness	Temperature	Timing	Time to pasteurize
Chicken	1 - 1.5"	62.0°C 143.5°F	1-3 hours	2 hours
Duck	1 - 1.5"	58.0°C 136.5°F	1-3 hours	2 hours
Turkey	1.5 - 2"	62.0°C 143.5°F	1.5-3 hours	2.5 hours

THE LEG

Darker and fattier than breast meat. Comprised of the drumstick (lower part) and the thigh (upper part). Duck and turkey legs perform best under longer cooking times - good things come to those who wait!

	Thickness	Temperature	Timing	Time to pasteurize
Chicken	1 - 1.5"	65.0°C 149.0°F	1.5-3 hours	2.5 hours
Duck	1 - 2"	70.0°C 158.0°F	8-12 hours	2 hours
Turkey	1 - 2"	70.0°C 158.0°F	8-12 hours	2 hours

DID YOU KNOW?

The chicken is the closest living relative of the T-Rex, and there are more chickens on the planet than people. Scared?

The longest recorded flight for a chicken is 301.5 feet. Despite appearances, turkeys can fly distances of up to a mile. Ducks are the best fliers and can fly hundreds of miles a day.

It's possible for a chicken to live without its head. Mike the Headless Chicken lived for 18 months without a head in 1945, went on tour and even featured in *Time* and *Life* magazines!

Thicknesss   Temperature   Timing   Time to pasteurize

CHICKEN *Noodle* SOUP

Noodle soups are a staple in the Far East, whether in the form of Japanese Ramen, Vietnamese Pho or Malaysian Curry Laksa.

You can reinvent the classic chicken noodle soup by applying the sous-vide technique to the chicken and egg. Glistening, juicy breast meat with yolk-coated slippery noodles is just pure bliss.

You can have this anytime - breakfast, lunch or dinner. It's light, healthy and reinvigorating.

Ingredients:

Chicken & Eggs
- 2 eggs
- 2 boneless chicken breasts

Noodles
- 300g (10 oz) fresh egg noodles
- 10ml (2 tsp) sesame oil

Soup
- 1.2 liter (5 cups) of chicken stock
- 180g (6 oz) baby pak choy, washed and trimmed

To Finish
- 2 sprigs of spring onions, finely chopped
- 1 red chili, chopped
- 5 shallots, finely sliced and deep fried (optional)

Method:

1 hour 10 minutes before
- Set Codlo to preheat water bath to 63°C (145°F) with 1 hour cooking time.
- Once target temperature is reached, place chicken breasts in bag, seal and submerge in water bath. Then, use a spoon to gently place 2 eggs in the water bath to cook as well.

10 minutes before
- Cook egg noodles as per pack instructions. Drain and toss it with some sesame oil, before distributing them amongst the serving bowls. Set aside.
- Bring the chicken stock to boil in a saucepan. Reduce heat to medium low and add in baby pak choy to cook for 3-5 minutes. Remove from heat.

TIP: Tossing the cooked noodles in a little bit of oil keeps the noodles smooth and separated even as it cools.

To plate
- Once the chicken and eggs are ready, remove chicken from pouch and pat dry. Slice the chicken breasts thinly and place them on top of the noodles.
- Carefully crack each egg gently on top of the noodles. Add some hot soup and baby pak choy to the noodles, topped with sprinkles of spring onion, chillies and deep fried shallots. Serve immediately.

⊘ CHEF'S TIP:

One of the benefits of sous-vide is that different items can be cooked together at the same temperature. At 63°C (145°F), you'll get juicy chicken breasts and slow cooked eggs with a thick gooey yolk - in one go.

Ingredients:

Chicken
- 4 boneless, skinless chicken breasts

Arrabiata Sauce
- 15ml (1 tbsp) olive oil
- 1/2 onion, chopped
- 4 garlic cloves, minced
- 2 fresh red chilies, de-seeded and finely chopped
- 12g (1 tbsp) brown sugar
- 400g (14 oz) canned chopped tomatoes
- 50ml (3 tbsp) tomato paste
- 50ml (3 tbsp) red wine
- 2g (1/2 tsp) black pepper
- 4g (1 tsp) dried basil

Pasta
- Salt, to taste
- 375g (13 oz) conchiglie (seashell pasta)

To Finish
- Parmesan cheese shavings

Pasta is a firm favorite, especially for midweek meals. It's simple, delicious and versatile. This technique works with any pasta sauce. With this sous-vide version, the cooked chicken breast portions are added into the thick sauce right at the end to a juicier, more succulent finish.

Method:

1 hour 15 minutes before
- Set Codlo to preheat water bath to 62°C (144°F) with 1 hour cooking time.
- Once target temperature is reached, seal the chicken breasts in bags and submerge them in the water bath.

20 minutes before
- Make the Arrabiata sauce: Heat olive oil in a large saucepan. Sauté onion and garlic for 5 minutes. Add in chilies, sugar, chopped tomatoes, tomato paste, red wine and black pepper. Bring to a boil, reduce heat to medium low to simmer uncovered for 15 minutes.
- While the sauce is simmering, bring a separate pot of salted water to boil. Cook pasta until al dente. Set aside.
- Once the sauce has reduced, add dried basil and salt to taste. Remove from heat and set aside.
- Once chicken is ready, pat them dry with kitchen towels and cut into bite-sized cubes.

TIP: If you have fresh basil at hand, roughly chop 20g (0.7 oz) of it to use as substitute for the dried ones.

To plate
- Add chicken and pasta into the warm Arrabiata sauce to toss and mix evenly. Serve immediately with Parmesan shavings.

Comments?
Air your thoughts to @codlo!

⊙ **CHEF'S TIP:**

You can also experiment with other pasta shapes. Smaller variants will cling on to more sauce!

CHICKEN & *Pea* RISOTTO

Ingredients:

Chicken
- 2 boneless, skin-on chicken breast

Risotto
- 15ml (1 tbsp) olive oil
- 1 onion, diced
- 400g (14oz) arborio rice
- 2 liter (8.5 cups) chicken or vegetable stock
- 50ml (3 tbsp) white wine
- Salt & black pepper
- 200g (7 oz) frozen peas
- 50ml cream (optional)
- 30ml (2 tbsp) oil

To Finish
- 60g (2 oz) parmesan, grated

Risotto is a versatile canvas for seasonal produce. It's great with vegetables, seafood and poultry, making it easy to create your own version once you've got the basics right. I like my risotto rich and creamy but still retaining a bit of chewiness, with separate, non-mushy grains.

Method:

1 hour 15 minutes before
- Set Codlo to preheat water bath to 62°C (144°F) with 1 hour cooking time. Once target temperature is reached, seal the chicken breasts in a bag and submerge in water bath.

35 minutes before
- Heat olive oil in a pan on medium heat. Add onions and fry until soft. Add the rice, stirring well for 2 minutes, before adding white wine and half of the stock.
- Simmer the mixture until reduced, adding in more stock each time the rice comes close to fully absorbing the liquid. Continue for 20-30 minutes whilst stirring until the rice is cooked al dente.
- Season with salt and black pepper. Stir in the peas and cream. Remove from heat once peas are cooked (around 2 min) and set aside.
- Once the chicken is ready, pat them dry with kitchen towels. Season with salt and pepper. Heat up oil in a heavy-based skillet, sear the chicken breasts skin side down on high heat for 30 seconds until crisp. Remove chicken from heat, slice them into portions.

To plate
- Spoon risotto onto serving bowl and top it with chicken slices. Sprinkle with Parmesan prior to serving.

◯ CHEF'S TIP:

The key to a great risotto is that it can't be rushed: go for medium heat and a gradual addition of stock, waiting for each addition to be absorbed into the rice before adding the next. This encourages release of starch which makes the risotto creamier.

HAINANESE *Chicken* RICE

Just ask anyone from the South East Asian region what Hainanese chicken rice is and chances are, most of them will just take you to try it. It's such a simple, yet beautifully executed dish - something you definitely should try making yourself.

A dish with a Chinese origin, it is traditionally cooked by steeping a whole chicken into a huge pot of water or stock at temperatures below boiling for a certain amount of time. This makes chicken rice a perfect candidate for sous-vide! I've detailed the recipe on a smaller scale using chicken thighs, but you can easily scale it up and serve it on a large plate, family style.

Have you tried this?
Let us know what you think on Twitter via @codlo!

Ingredients:

Chicken
- 600g (21 oz) boneless chicken thighs
- 10ml (2 tsp) sesame oil

Rice
- 30ml (2 tbsp) sesame oil
- 50g (1.8 oz) ginger, minced
- 5 cloves of garlic, minced
- 40g (1.4 oz) chicken fat
- 500g (17.6 oz) jasmine rice
- 850ml (3.5 cups) chicken stock

Ginger Chili Sauce
- 5 fresh red chilies, chopped
- 30g (1 oz) ginger, skinned and sliced
- 3 cloves of garlic
- 4g (1 tsp) sugar
- 2g (1/2 tsp) salt
- 5ml (1 tsp) lime juice
- 30ml (2 tbsp) chicken stock

Sesame-soy Sauce
- 30ml (2 tbsp) sesame oil
- 60ml (4 tbsp) light soy sauce

To Finish
- 1 cucumber, sliced thinly
- Coriander, chopped

Method:

1 hour 45 minutes before
- Set Codlo to preheat water bath to 65°C (149°F) with 1 hour 30 minutes cooking time.
- Once the target temperature is reached, seal the chicken thighs with 2 teaspoons of sesame oil in a bag and submerge them in the water bath.

45 minutes before
- For the rice: heat up the sesame oil in a heavy-based pot. Stir-fry ginger, garlic and chicken fat until aromatic. Add rice, stir for 5 minutes before adding the chicken stock.
- Once the mixture boils, reduce heat to medium. Simmer with the lid on for 30 minutes until cooked. Add more water if necessary.
- When the chicken is cooked, submerge the bag containing the chicken in a pot of ice cold water for 15 minutes. Remove from bag and cut them into bite-sized pieces.
- For the chili sauce: chop and mix the chilies, ginger, garlic, sugar, salt and lime juice in a blender. Add chicken stock and season to taste. Set aside.
- Prepare the sesame-soy sauce simply by mixing sesame oil and light soy sauce. Set aside.

To plate
- Drizzle some sesame-soy sauce generously over a portion of chicken, topped with some chopped coriander. Serve with rice, sliced cucumber and chili sauce.

○ CHEF'S TIP:

Shocking the meat in ice-cold water firms it up and creates a gelatinous layer between the skin and meat.

had my first Caribbean dish - Jerk Chicken - in the UK. Although I wasn't in the sunny Caribbean, I was nonetheless mind blown by its cuisine. It has flavors that pack a punch and tastes so refreshingly different despite using familiar spices. That got me started on my spice exploration journey and I haven't looked back since.

I've updated my original recipe for a sous-vide version. It's especially awesome for barbecues where you can finish the chicken on the grill. With this, you can easily be the one who blows everyone out of the water at your next BBQ party!

Ingredients:

Jerk Chicken
- 8 chicken thighs
- 3 garlic cloves, minced
- 12g (1 tbsp) chili flakes
- 6g (1/2 tbsp) chili powder
- 12g (1 tbsp) brown sugar
- 12g (1 tbsp) salt
- 4g (1 tsp) each: ground allspice, cumin
- 2g (1/2 tsp) each: ground cinnamon, nutmeg and dried thyme
- 30ml (2 tbsp) peanut oil

Rice
- 7.5ml (1/2 tbsp) lime juice
- 450g (16 oz) long grain rice
- 360ml (1.5 cups) water
- 400ml (1.7 cups) coconut milk
- 4g (1 tsp) paprika
- 3 x 120g (4 oz) canned beans, drained (borlotti, flageolet and black beans)
- 5g (1 tsp) salt
- 50g (1.8 oz) canned sweet corn, drained
- Salt
- 30ml (2 tbsp) peanut oil

Method:

1 day before
- Combine garlic, chili flakes, chili powder, sugar, salt, allspice, cumin, cinnamon, nutmeg, thyme, peanut oil and lime juice in a large bowl. Stir to make a smooth paste.
- Add chicken thighs to the bowl and rub the paste onto the meat evenly. Cover and leave to marinate for 6 hours, or overnight.

TIP: This may be a long list of spices, but it's also an opportunity to build up your spice rack and try this flavorful Caribbean twist to chicken!

1 hour 45 minutes before
- Set Codlo to preheat water bath to 65°C (149°F) with 1 hour 30 minutes cooking time. Once the target temperature is reached, seal chicken thighs in a bag and submerge them in the water bath.

30 minutes before
- Bring rice and water to a near boil over high heat, stirring occasionally. Lower heat to medium. Stir in coconut milk and paprika. Simmer for 7 minutes until most of the liquid is absorbed. Reduce heat to low and heat for 10 minutes with the lid on. Your rice should be dry when done.
- Remove from heat, allow the rice to rest for 10 minutes. Mix in salt, sweet corn and the various beans, set aside.
- Once chicken is ready, pat them dry with kitchen towels, season them with salt. Heat up oil in a heavy-based skillet. Sear the chicken skin side down on high heat for 1 minute until crisp. Flip over and cook for another 10 seconds. Remove from heat and set aside.

TIP: Feel free to use your preferred mixture of beans here. Butter, pinto, cannellini and broad beans are good substitutes.

To plate
- Serve 1-2 chicken thighs per person on a bed of rice with beans.

MALAYSIAN *Chicken* SATAY

Need any more tips?
Let us know on
Twitter via @codlo!

This skewered delight is the quintessential Asian street food. However, satay is often misrepresented globally - the marinade or sauces never quite seem to be the same as the original. This recipe is practical with easily available ingredients yet authentic tasting. It's great for starters and crowds and you can make this any time of the year as barbequing is optional. Just a frying pan would do!

Ingredients:

Chicken & Marinade
- 1/2 yellow onion, chopped
- 16g (4 tsp) palm sugar
- 8g (2 tsp) each (powder form): paprika, chili, coriander, turmeric, cumin
- 5ml (1 tsp) vegetable oil
- 4g (1 tsp) salt
- 600g (21 oz) deboned chicken thighs, skin reserved

Satay Sauce
- Vegetable oil
- 3 shallots, skinned
- 2 garlic cloves, skinned
- 2 fresh red chilies, head removed
- 15g (0.5 oz) ginger, skinned and chopped
- 2g (1/2 tsp) turmeric powder
- 12g (1 tbsp) coriander powder
- 100ml (0.4 cups) water
- 12g (1 tbsp) palm / brown sugar
- 30g (2 tbsp) crunchy peanut butter
- 2g (1/2 tsp) salt
- 60ml (4 tbsp) coconut milk

For the Grill
- 20 wooden skewers
- Vegetable oil
- 30ml (2 tbsp) honey
- 30 ml (2 tbsp) oil
- 2 cucumbers, cut into chunks

Method:

1 day before
- For the marinade paste: pulse the onion in a food processor until fine. Transfer to a large bowl. Mix in sugar, paprika, chili, coriander, turmeric, cumin, vegetable oil and salt to make a paste.
- Cut chicken thighs and skin into bite-sized chunks and mix evenly with marinade paste. Cover and refrigerate for 6 hours, or overnight.

TIP: This may be a long list of spices, but easily found in most grocery stores.

2 hours before
- Set Codlo to preheat water bath to 65°C (149°F) with 1 hour 30 minutes cooking time.
- Once the target temperature is reached, seal chicken thighs in a bag and submerge them in the water bath.

30 minutes before
- Heat 2 tbsp vegetable oil in a saucepan on medium. Pulse shallots, garlic, chilies, ginger, turmeric and coriander powder in a food processor until it forms a paste. Fry the paste for 5 minutes until aromatic.
- Add in water, sugar, peanut butter, salt and increase heat to bring to a boil. Reduce heat to simmer gently, while stirring occasionally. Add coconut milk, adjust seasoning to taste and simmer for another 5 minutes. Turn off heat, set aside.

TIP: The satay sauce will thicken further as it cools down.

15 minutes before
- Once the chicken is ready, pat dry with kitchen towels. Thread the meat and skin alternately through the skewers.
- Heat 2 tbsp vegetable oil in a large heavy-based pan. Whisk honey and oil in a separate bowl and brush the mixture on the meat on each skewer. Sear the skewers quickly for 10 seconds each side until brown. Do this in batches and replenish oil if needed.

TIP: Alternatively, it's fantastic grilled or BBQ briefly for a smokier flavor.

To plate
- Place satay skewers on a plate with cucumber. Serve with satay sauce.

DUCK BREAST *with* GARLICKY PAK CHOY

I am a huge, huge fan of the crispy roast duck in Hong Kong or Chinese restaurants. Duck is best served medium for a succulent feel. It's a great dish to try when you first host a sit-down dinner party, as it's designed to be minimum fuss with maximum impact.

Ingredients:

Duck Breast
- 2 duck breast
- 4g (1 tsp) five spice powder
- Salt

For the Frying Pan
- Salt & black pepper
- 3 cloves of garlic, minced

Garlicky Pak Choy
- 250g (9 oz) pak choy, washed, sliced lengthwise
- 30ml (2 tbsp) light soy sauce
- 30ml (2 tbsp) clear honey
- Salt

○ CHEF'S TIP:

Be careful when browning the duck skin. There will be lots of fat rendering out, sizzling hot and popping.

Method:

1 hour 15 minutes before
- Set Codlo to preheat water bath to 57°C (135°F) with 1 hour cooking time.
- With a fork, gently prick the duck skin without piercing into the meat. Repeat for the whole skin area. Rub the meat with five spice powder and some salt on the duck skin.
- Once target temperature is reached, seal the duck breasts in a bag and submerge in the water bath.

TIP: Medium is recommended here to avoid chewiness. With sous-vide, it may look pink, but taste perfect. Try it and see!

10 minutes before
- Once the duck breasts are ready, pat them dry with kitchen towels. Season duck skin with some salt and black pepper.
- Heat up a heavy-based skillet without oil. Sear the duck breast skin-side down on medium heat for 5 minutes until golden and crispy. Turn the duck breast over and cook for 30 seconds. Remove from heat, set aside to cool before slicing.
- Using the same pan, brown the minced garlic briefly in the duck fat. Set aside.
- Place pak choy in the steamer and steam for 3 minutes until tender. Set aside.
- Mix honey and soy sauce in a bowl, heat in the microwave for 1 minute until bubbling and reduced.

To plate
- Place pak choy on the top part of the plate, lightly season with salt and sprinkle minced garlic on top. Brush a large dash of sauce in the center and place sliced duck pieces on top of it.

Ingredients:

Duck Breasts
- 4 duck breasts

Accompaniments
- 50g (1.8 oz) butter
- 200g (7 oz) chestnut mushrooms, quartered
- 250g (9 oz) spinach leaves
- Salt, to taste

Seasoning
- 20ml (4 tsp) light soy sauce
- 20ml (4 tsp) honey
- 40ml (2.5 tbsp) sunflower oil
- 10ml (2 tsp) white vinegar
- 100g (3.5 oz) roasted pumpkin seeds

Enjoyed this?
Tweet your experience to @codlo!

Duck breast is always awesome with sweet sauces. But here's something a little different - it's light on sauce and focuses on the pure gamey flavor of the meat. The sauce also has a more savory and tangy note to it for those who fancy something new.

Method:

1 hour 15 minutes before
- Set Codlo to preheat water bath to 57°C (135°F) with 1 hour cooking time.
- Score the duck skin carefully with a knife without cutting into the meat. Once the target temperature is reached, seal the duck breasts in a bag and submerge in the water bath.

15 minutes before
- Once the duck breasts are ready, pat them dry with kitchen towels. Heat a heavy-based skillet without oil. Sear the duck breasts skin-side down on medium heat until golden (5 min). Do this in batches if necessary. Turn the duck breast over and cook for 30 seconds. Remove from heat, set aside.
- In a separate pan, melt the butter and sauté the mushrooms until aromatic. Remove pan from heat, add in spinach to wilt by stirring quickly. Season to taste with salt.
- Whisk light soy sauce, honey, sunflower oil and white vinegar in a bowl. Test and adjust taste to your preference.

To plate
- Sprinkle some salt on duck breast prior to slicing them. Place sliced duck in the center of the plate, spoon some mushroom mixture around it.
- Scatter a pinch (or two) of roasted pumpkin seeds and drizzle a teaspoon of dressing. Serve immediately.

Duck confit is pretty magical - a lot of it is just letting time work things out by itself. A long salt cure coupled with slow cooking, finished with a quick sear in a pan to crisp the skin in its own fat - gives you this amazing dinner with little effort. Here are some alternative time/temp combinations. The recipe opts for a juicier finish with a slower cook:

- **75°C (167°F) for 10 hours**
- **80°C (176°F) for 8 hours**

Ingredients:

Duck
- 2 duck legs
- 100g (3.5 oz) of salt
- 1 bay leaf, crumbled
- Sprig of Thyme
- 30ml (2 tbsp) of duck fat

Accompaniments
- 300g (10 oz) spinach leaves
- Black pepper
- 30ml (2 tbsp) olive oil

⬥ CHEF'S TIP:

The duck legs can keep for another 3 days in the refrigerator in its unopened pouch, until ready for use. Posh midweek dinners made possible!

Method:

1 day before
- To cure the duck: add crumbled bay leaf and thyme to salt. Place the duck legs in a deep dish. Rub salt mixture on them vigorously. Leave it to cure, uncovered, in the refrigerator for 10-12 hours.

TIP: You can cure the legs for up to 2 days. The color of the meat will be more intense and the excess salt needs to be properly rinsed out later.

12 hours 30 minutes before
- Set Codlo to preheat water bath to 70°C(158°F) with 12 hours cooking time.
- Thoroughly rinse off all the salt from the duck legs with water. Once target temperature is reached, seal each duck leg in a bag with 1 tbsp of duck fat. Submerge bag in water bath.

10 minutes before
- When the duck is ready, reserve the liquid in the pouch. Pat dry the duck with kitchen towels. Heat a heavy-based skillet without oil. Sear the duck legs skin-side down on medium heat until golden (3-5 min). Turn the duck legs over and cook for 30 seconds. Remove from heat, set aside.
- Bring the reserved liquid to a boil until slightly reduced for the jus, set aside.
- In a separate pan, heat olive oil on high heat. Add spinach leaves to cook briefly until just wilted. Lightly season with black pepper.

TIPS: It's OK to go without salting the spinach here as well, since the sauce will make up for it.

To plate
- Place duck legs on top of a bed of spinach, with a drizzling of jus.

PORK

Pork is quite similar to poultry in terms of cooking methods. We take it a step further here by introducing the brining technique (see the Techniques & Equipment section for more information). Although not necessary for pork (or poultry), brining improves moisture retention and can enhance bite and mouthfeel for leaner cuts such as tenderloin (fillet) and chops.

Pork belly is a firm favorite and we've got three recipes here using pork bellies in various ways. How they differ is mainly in the finishing steps: in general, for large blocks of pork belly, we recommend quick-chilling, drying and flattening the skin under a weight for crispier skin. Crisping the skin from cold using the grill also allows the skin to crisp up without overcooking the meat. Alternatively you could always choose to deep fry or pan fry it, it's up to you!

On the other hand, pork shoulder is a leaner, tougher cut that benefits from a longer and slower cooking. The pulled pork recipe here is just one way to showcase how tender and juicy it can be, not much fancy additions needed. Just great ingredients, cooked perfectly; great for feeding a crowd.

CODLO'S SOUS-VIDE *Guide* TO PORK

ALL ABOUT PORK CUTS...

The back section along both sides of the backbone. Includes the tenderloin, the leanest and most tender cut. Also provides the back ribs.

(t) = Thin Cuts 1.0 - 1.5 inches
(T) = Thick Cuts up to 2.5 inches

- **(t)** Tenderloin / Fillet
- **(t)** Chops and Steak
- **(T)** Boneless Roasts or Joints
- **(T)** Baby Back Ribs

A tougher cut, cooking low and slow makes the meat more tender.

- **(t)** Leg Cutlet
- **(T)** Leg Joints

A very versatile cut. The pork shoulder provides the highest level of marbling, perfect for roasting or braising.

- **(T)** Shoulder Joint
- **(t)** Shoulder Steak

Belly pork is wonderfully rich - and value for money! Cooking low and slow reduces the fat and results in luscious and succulent indulgence.

- **(T)** Spare Ribs
- **(T)** Belly Joint

GIVE A FORK ABOUT YOUR PORK

- There are about a **billion** pigs in the world at any one time.
- Pork tenderloin cuts are **almost as lean as skinless chicken breast.**
- Weight-wise, pork is by far the **most widely consumed** meat, with about 100 tonnes eaten annually.

(t) *Cooking Thin Cuts of Pork*

PINK & MOIST	TRADITIONAL STYLE
🌡 56-58°C / 133-136°F	🌡 60°C / 140°F
🕐 1.5-2.0 hours	🕐 1.5-2.0 hours
⭐P 2.5 hours	⭐P 2.5 hours

(T) *Cooking Thick Cuts of Pork*

SOFT & MOIST	TRADITIONAL STYLE
🌡 60-65°C / 140-149°F	🌡 75°C / 167°F
🕐 24-48 hours	🕐 8-12 hours
⭐P 4 hours	⭐P 2.5 hours

Temperature

Timing

Time to pasteurize

PORK *Tenderloin* WITH MASH AND MUSTARD-CIDER SAUCE

A very similar experience here with chicken breast in terms of transformation under sous-vide, though not surprising if you knew that pork tenderloin is almost as lean as chicken breast. We cook it slightly on the pink side to allow a little more **headroom for pan-frying** later. Pan-frying is **optional though**. It's excellent and extra juicy **served immediately** too - our go-to quick **and fuss-free** comfort food.

Ingredients:

Pork
- 350g (12 oz) pork fillet

Mash
- 350g (12 oz) potatoes, peeled and coarsely chopped
- 28g (1 oz) butter
- 60ml (4 tbsp) milk
- Salt and black pepper

Accompaniments
- 200g (7 oz) purple sprouting broccoli

For the Frying Pan
- Salt
- 30ml (2 tbsp) oil
- 2g (1/2 tsp) salt

Mustard-Cider Sauce
- 150ml (0.6 cups) cider
- 15ml (1 tbsp) wholegrain mustard
- 60ml (4 tbsp) single cream

Comments?
Let us know on Twitter @codlo!

Method:

2 hours before
- Set Codlo to preheat water bath to 57°C (135°F) with 1 hour 30 minutes cooking time. Once target temperature is reached, seal pork fillets in a bag and submerge it in the water bath.

TIP: Pork tenderloins tend to come in long strips, if necessary, cut it in half to fit the bag.

15 minutes before
- Cook potatoes in a pot of salted boiling water for 15 minutes until tender, drain.
- In a separate saucepan, warm milk and butter over low heat until butter melts. Add milk mixture to potatoes gradually and mash until smooth. Season with salt and black pepper to taste. Set aside.
- Blanch the purple sprouting broccoli for 2-3 minutes in a pot of salted, boiling water. Shock them in ice water, drain and set aside.
- Once the pork is done, remove from bag and pat dry with kitchen towels. Heat oil in a heavy-based skillet. Season the pork with salt and sear the fillets evenly to brown in about 45 seconds. Set pork aside and slice into pieces.
- Reduce heat to medium. Deglaze the same pan with cider and let it reduce slightly. Add mustard and single cream, simmer sauce for 2 minutes while stirring. Set aside.

To plate
- Place a dollop of mash in the center of the plate, topped with a few slices of tender pork fillet. Drizzle some mustard-cider sauce over it and place some purple sprouting broccoli on the side. Serve immediately.

CHEF'S TIP:

Don't worry if the meat is still rather pale after the brief pan-fry. All the flavor will be subsequently captured when deglazing the pan for your sauce.

PORK *Chops* WITH SPINACH AND MUSHROOM SAUCE

Pork chops are easy to overcook and you usually see them in thin slices for even cooking. With sous-vide you can get thicker (up to 3.8cm / 1.5 inches), bone-in ones for a rustic presentation and have more leeway for browning the meat too. I serve it with spinach and a simple mushroom sauce in this recipe, but they are great with tangy or creamy sauces too.

Ingredients:

Pork
- 2 pork chops, about 300g (10 oz) each

Spinach
- 15ml (1 tbsp) olive oil
- 300g (10 oz) spinach leaves
- Salt and black pepper

For the Frying Pan
- 30ml (2 tbsp) oil

Mushroom Sauce
- 15g (1 tbsp) butter
- 150g (5 oz) mushrooms, chopped
- 250ml (1 cup) single cream
- 2g (1/2 tsp) wholegrain mustard
- Salt and black pepper

Method:

2 hours before
- Set Codlo to preheat water bath to 57°C (135°F) with 1 hour 30 minutes cooking time. Once target temperature is reached, seal pork chops in a bag and submerge it in the water bath.

10 minutes before
- Heat olive oil on medium heat. Add spinach leaves to cook briefly until just wilted. Season with salt and pepper. Set aside.
- Once the pork is done, remove from bag and pat dry with kitchen towels. Heat oil in a heavy-based skillet until near smoking. Sear the fillets on all sides to brown for about 15 seconds per side. Set aside.
- For the sauce: melt butter in hot pan and fry the mushrooms until soften and brown. Remove pan from heat briefly to stir in cream and mustard. Return pan to stove and cook on medium-low heat and simmer until desired consistency. Season with salt and pepper to taste.

To plate
- Arrange spinach on the side of each plate. Place a pork chop in the middle and drizzle with some mushroom sauce. Serve immediately.

CHEF'S TIP:

The pork chops are deliberately cooked with a hint of pink so there's a little more leeway when browning the meat later on, to minimize the risk of overcooking.

PORK *Belly* BUNS

These pork buns are great finger food for your party, or as starters if it's a sit-down affair. It's quite a crowd pleaser so it's best to make more than one portion per person, as many will come back and ask for more!

The sous-vide version strikes the perfect balance of moist and tender interior with crispy cracklings. It does require some advance planning but it's mostly set-and-

forget, making the last minute prep dead easy.

Here are some alternative time/temp combinations for pork belly cuts with 3.8-6.4cm (1.5-2.5 inches) thicknesses. Try them and see what you prefer:

- 60°C (140°F) for 48 hours
- 65°C (149°F) for 36 hours
- 80°C (176°F) for 12 hours

Ingredients:

Pork
- 600g (20 oz) slab of pork belly, skin-on
- Salt

Cucumber Relish
- 1 whole cucumber
- 12g (3 tsp) sugar
- 4g (1 tsp) salt

To Finish
- 12 mini plain steamed buns
- 100ml (0.4 cups) Hoisin sauce

Need another tip?
Just shout out to @ codlo on Twitter!

● CHEF'S TIP:

Choose leaner cuts of pork belly for best results.

Method:

2 days before
- Set Codlo to preheat water bath to 70°C (158°F) with 24 hours cooking time. Once target temperature is reached, seal the pork belly in a bag and submerge in the water bath.

1 day before before
- Once it's cooked, rapid chill the sealed bag containing the pork in an ice bath. Place the unopened pouch containing the pork belly skin side down between two baking trays and a weight on top to flatten the skin. Refrigerate for at least 3 hours, or overnight.

TIP: The goal here is to get the meat nice and flat for even crisping of the skin later.

30 minutes before
- Remove the chilled pork from the bag. Rub salt on the skin generously. Cut the pork into 1cm (2/3 inch) thick portions with the same width as the buns. Preheat broiler to 250°C (482°F). Place the sliced pork together skin side up and wrap tightly with aluminum foil on all sides, except the skin. Grill for 10-12 minutes until crispy.
- Meanwhile, shred the cucumber with a grater. Mix in salt and sugar, set aside.
- Steam the buns for 5-8 minutes until soft and fluffy, do this in batches if necessary. Slice the buns 3/4 open, leaving a 'hinge'.

TIP: It's best to slice your pork when it's chilled. The meat is firmer when cold, allowing you to cut without it falling apart. For the plain steamed buns, look for the ones shaped like a sock-puppet mouth, which can be bought from Asian supermarkets - you won't need to slice them open then!

To plate
- To assemble: spread a thin layer of Hoisin sauce on the base of each bun. Place a piece of pork belly and top it with some grated cucumber. Serve immediately.

CRISPY *Pork* BELLY WITH CHERRY TOMATOES, CARROT PURÉE AND CIDER GLAZE

nstead of the usual pairing with apple, the sweetness and slight acidity of the cherry tomatoes works like a charm here, giving a burst of flavor to the dish. This dish is also brightened up with the visually stunning carrot purée and you'll have fun learning how to "swoosh" the purée using the back of the spoon here. Be confident and decisive when swooshing, practice makes perfect!

Ingredients:

Pork & Brine
- 2.5 liter (10.5 cups) of water
- 125g (4.4 oz) salt
- 75g (2.6 oz) sugar
- 800g pork belly with skin
- 2g (½ tsp) garlic powder
- 2g (½ tsp) black pepper

Carrot Purée
- 250g fresh carrots, diced
- 90ml (6 tbsp) double cream
- 30g (1 oz) of butter
- Salt
- Oil

Cider Jus
- 60ml (1/4 cup) dry cider
- 180ml (3/4 cup) chicken stock
- Salt and black pepper
- 8 cherry tomatoes, halved

Method:

3 days before
- Dissolve salt and sugar in a large bowl of water to prepare the brine (5% salt, 3% sugar). Brine the pork belly in the liquid, refrigerated for 6 hours, or overnight.

2 days before
- Set Codlo to preheat water bath to 60°C (158°F) with 36 hours cooking time.
- Remove meat from brine, rinse and dry with paper towels. Rub garlic powder and black pepper evenly onto the meat, except the skin.
- Once the target temperature is reached, seal the pork belly in a bag and submerge in the water bath.

12 hours before
- Once cooked, chill the pork in the bag in ice water.
- Place the unopened pouch with the pork belly skin side down between two baking trays, with a weight on top to flatten the skin. Refrigerate until use.

40 minutes before
- Boil the carrots until tender. Drain and purée with the cream and butter. Season well and set aside, keeping warm.
- Remove the pork from the bag, cut into 4 equal portions.
- Heat up some oil in a heavy-based pan. Sear the pork belly slices for about 30 seconds per side, longer for the skin. Set aside.
- To make the cider jus: deglaze the same pan with cider and stock. Boil rapidly until reduced and syrupy. Adjust seasoning to taste. Set aside.

To plate
- Using the back of a spoon, 'swoosh' a spoonful of carrot purée at a corner of the plate.
- Position the pork on the purée and scatter cherry tomatoes. Add a spoonful of cider jus. Serve immediately.

CHINESE *BBQ* PORK (CHAR SIU)

This recipe took quite a few tries to get right - endless rounds of testing various cuts, time/temperature combinations, marinade compositions and finishing methods! It's common for char siu to be dry and overcooked in restaurants, compensated with a very sweet and salty sauce. This sous-vide version, however, can stand proudly on its own.

Given the smaller cut, thinner strips and brining process, the recipe goes for a lower temperature range to prevent it from drying out. If you prefer it less pink (but drier), try 63°C (145°F) for 1.5 hours for pork belly cuts 2.5-3.8cm (1-1.5 inches) thick.

Ingredients:

Char Siu Marinade
- 2g (1/2 tsp) five spice powder
- 2g (1/2 tsp) white pepper
- 15ml (1 tbsp) Shao Xing wine (or brandy)
- 15ml (1 tbsp) dark soy sauce
- 30ml (2 tbsp) light soy sauce
- 30ml (2 tbsp) Hoi Sin sauce
- 60ml (4 tbsp) sugar
- 700ml (3 cups) water

Pork
- 500g (17.5 oz) skinless pork belly, cut into long strips about 2.5cm (1 inch) wide

Others
- Ice-cold water
- Vegetable oil

Enjoyed this?
Tweet your favorites to @codlo!

Method:

12 hours before
- Mix five spice powder, white pepper, Shao Xing wine, sugar, Hoi Sin, dark and light soy sauce in a bowl. Microwave the mixture for a minute to dissolve the sugar. Reserve half, set aside to cool before storing it in the refrigerator.
- Place the other half of the warm mixture in a huge bowl, stir in 700ml (3 cups) water. Soak the pork belly strips in the brine for 6 hours or overnight in the fridge.

TIP: Choose leaner cuts of pork belly for best results.

2 hours 30 minutes before
- Set Codlo to preheat water bath to 57°C (135°F) with 2 hours cooking time. Once target temperature is reached, remove pork belly from brine. Seal them in a bag and submerge it in the water bath. Reserve excess marinade for later use.

15 minutes before
- Bring the reserved marinade to boil until thick and syrupy, set aside to cool.
- Once the pork belly is ready, rapidly chill the bag in ice-cold water for 5-10 minutes. Heat up a heavy-based frying pan with vegetable oil on high heat.
- Remove pork from the bag, pat dry with kitchen towel. Brush the warm marinade on all sides of the meat. Sear each pork strip quickly for 3-5 seconds a side until it caramelizes and is slightly charred. Set aside.

TIP: Grilling or using a blowtorch to char the meat briefly works too. Given the sweet marinade, sear the pork quickly to prevent burning.

To plate
- Slice the pork thinly. Serve immediately with rice or noodles.

☺ CHEF'S TIP:
The thin pork slices can dry out if left out too long. Serve them fresh!

PULLED *Pork* WITH RED ONION PICKLE AND MASH

Who doesn't like pulled pork? It's super versatile, works for burritos, buns, salads, or even on its own. **Dead easy to make with sous-vide too!**

I use pork shoulder for this recipe - a tougher cut that requires a longer cooking time to make it tender. With tougher cuts, you have a wider range of time and temperature combinations to try for the exact finish you prefer. This recipe goes for the middle ground with 70°C (158°F) for 24 hours. Here are some alternative settings for pork shoulders up to 3.8-7cm (1.5-2.8 inches) in thickness:

- 63°C (145°F) for 48 hours
- 80°C (176°F) for 12 hours

Ingredients:

Pork & Seasoning
- 1kg (2.2 lbs) boneless pork shoulder, skin removed
- 8g (2 tsp) salt
- 24g (2 tbsp) brown sugar
- 12g (1 tbsp) paprika
- 6g (1/2 tbsp) garlic powder

Onion Pickles
- 2 red onions, thinly sliced
- 360ml (1.5 cups) white vinegar
- 100g (3.5 oz) sugar
- 4g (1 tsp) salt
- 5 cloves
- 1/2 cinnamon stick
- 1 star anise
- 4g (1 tsp) red chili flakes
- 20g (4 tsp) salt

Mash
- 1kg (2.2 lbs) potatoes, peeled and quartered
- 45g (1.5 oz) butter
- 237ml (1 cup) milk or cream, warmed
- Salt and black pepper

To Finish
- Toasted bread
- BBQ sauce

Method:

1 day before
- Set Codlo to preheat water bath to 70°C (158°F) with 24 hours cooking time. Mix the seasonings (salt, sugar, paprika, garlic powder) and rub into the pork.
- Once target temperature is reached, seal the pork in a bag and submerge it in the water bath.
- In a saucepan, bring the white vinegar, sugar, salt, cloves, cinnamon stick, star anise and chili flakes to boil.
- Reduce heat to simmer for 2 minutes. Add in sliced onions and simmer for 3 minutes. Remove from heat and let it cool completely. Transfer the onions and the liquid into a jar. Refrigerate until use.

TIPS: Weighing down the meat with a plate when sous-vide cooking will ensure that it's submerged at all times. The pickle will keep for 3 weeks refrigerated, but tastes best in the first week.

20 minutes before
- Boil the potatoes gently in a large pot of salted water until tender (easily cut by fork). Drain and set aside for 5 minutes until steam has evaporated.
- Place potatoes in a bowl. Slowly mash with a fork until lump-free. Add butter and milk (or cream) gradually, checking the consistency as you mash. Season with salt and black pepper to taste and set aside.

TIPS: For a slightly cheesy mash, add 75g (3 oz) creamed cheese (room temperature). Try not to use an electric whisk or food processor as it tends to ruin the texture.

To plate
- Once the pork is ready, remove from bag onto a large chopping board or mixing bowl. Shred the meat with a fork and place in a bowl. Lightly toss it with some BBQ sauce before serving it with red onion pickle, mash and bread.

⊙ CHEF'S TIP:

Choose Yukon Gold or Desiree potatoes for the best mash texture.

SEAFOOD

Delicate ingredients such as fish and shellfish are prone to overcooking, rendering them rubbery and (too) firm. The gentle sous-vide treatment brings out the best in them so do make sure you get fresh and high quality seafood for these recipes. You'll get to try amazing new textures too, such as a lightly cooked, buttery medium-rare salmon that is slightly flaky yet very tender.

Seafood is an easy ingredient to master with sous-vide as they cook quicker and have less time and temperature variation overall. This gives you the opportunity to be more creative and arty about food plating and presentation.

When plating however, make sure you handle with care as seafood can be super fragile and tender when it's ready to eat!

CODLO'S SOUS-VIDE *Guide* TO SEAFOOD

THE FRUITS OF THE SEA

THE SEAFOOD SOUS-VIDE RULE OF THUMB:

43°C (109°F) rare
50°C (122°F) medium rare
60°C (140°F) medium

20 minutes for 1/2 inch thickness.
30 minutes for 1 inch thickness.

Note that the times above are not pasteurized times and therefore should not be served to immuno-compromised individuals.

To pasteurize fish and shellfish (up to 1 inch thick), the quickest way is to cook them to medium at 60°C (140°F) for 1.5 hour.

LOBSTER, SHRIMP & SCALLOPS

Shelled, 52°C, 20-30 minutes at maximum.

LEAN FISH:

Examples are cod, haddock, plaice, hake, lemon sole, monk fish, pollock, mullet, red snapper, sea bass, sea bream, turbot, whiting. Great cooked to medium rare at 47°C-50°C for 20-30 minutes, depending on thickness.

OILY FISH:

Examples are tuna, trout, swordfish and salmon**. They can be enjoyed rare at 43°C for a different experience, most people like them medium rare at 47°C-50°C. For those who prefer it more 'done,' go for medium at 55°C-60°C. Again, cook for 20-30 minutes, depending on thickness.

** For salmon, an extra brining step is necessary before cooking sous-vide. This prevents the secretion of white protein (albumin) when cooked, firms up the fish for easier handling and preserves the vibrant orange color even after it's cooked.

2 BADASS CRUSTACEANS YOU DIDN'T KNOW ABOUT

THE MANTIS SHRIMP

The mantis shrimp has claws with an incredibly fast and powerful strike, launching with the velocity of a bullet, capable of breaking aquarium glass.

THE PISTOL SHRIMP

The pistol shrimp can deliver an explosive attack hotter than the surface of the sun and loud enough to rupture a human ear drum.

Temperature

Timing

Time to pasteurize

CLASSIC PRAWN *Cocktail*

C all me old fashioned, but I love this retro British invention as it's fun to make. If you're planning a dinner party and are already frazzled, this would be the perfect starter to go for - it's easy yet looks impressive. It's versatile presentation-wise and can be served on a plate or something tiny like a shot glass - we used martini glasses here. One rule though, get fresh, high-quality prawns for this as it's the star of this dish!

Ingredients:

Prawns
- 350g (12 oz) large shrimps, shelled, deveined
- 15g (1 tbsp) butter

Cocktail Filling
- 1 gem lettuce, shredded
- 80g (2.8 oz) cucumber, shredded

Marie Rose Sauce
- 60ml (4 tbsp) mayonnaise
- 15ml (1 tbsp) tomato ketchup
- Juice of 1/2 lemon
- 5ml (1 tsp) Tabasco
- 2g (1/2 tsp) paprika
- Black pepper

To Finish
- 30g (1 oz) watercress
- Paprika
- Lemon wedges

Method:

25 minutes before
- Set Codlo to preheat water bath to 52°C (125°F) with 15 minutes cooking time. Once target temperature is reached, seal shrimps in a bag with butter and submerge it in the water bath.

5 minutes before
- Once prawns are ready, quick chill the (unopened) pouch in ice-cold water to cool for 5 minutes. Remove prawns from bag, pat dry with kitchen towel.
- Layer the glasses with lettuce and cucumber.
- Make the Marie Rose sauce by combining mayonnaise, ketchup, lemon juice, Tabasco, paprika and black pepper in a bowl. Set aside.

To plate
- Add a dollop of Marie Rose sauce on top of the bed of vegetables, topped with some prawns. Sprinkle with paprika and add some watercress on the side. Serve with a lemon wedge each, to be squeezed upon eating.

✪ CHEF'S TIP:

Iceberg lettuce is a good substitute for gem lettuce.

Did you know that about 150 years ago lobster was considered "trash food"? Lobsters were in full abundance and much larger then. Initially deemed only worthy to use as fertilizers and fish bait, it was later served to prisoners and treated as low-price canned food. How ironic! The world's pretty different now and if you're cooking lobsters for that special occasion, sous-vide would be the perfect technique to get it cooked just right.

Ingredients:

Lobster Tail
- 360g (12 oz) lobster tail
- 30g (1 oz) butter

Linguine
- 180g (6 oz) linguine
- 15ml (1 tbsp) olive oil
- 2 cloves of garlic, finely chopped
- 400ml (14 oz) can of Lobster Bisque soup
- 2g (1/2 tsp) grated lemon zest
- 15g (0.5 oz) chopped chives
- Salt and black pepper, to taste

Like this one?
Tweet us at @codlo and share your experience!

Method:

30 min before
- Set Codlo to preheat waterbath to 52°C (125°F) with 20 min cooking time. Once target temperature is reached, place lobster tails in a bag with some butter. Seal and submerge the bag in the waterbath.

10 min before
- Bring a large pot of salted water to boil and cook the linguine until al dente. Drain and set aside.
- Heat up olive up in a pan. Add in garlic, fry until fragrant for 1 min. Reduce heat to low and pour in the soup to simmer for 5 min. Remove pan from heat.
- Once lobster is ready, gently remove from bag, pat dry and slice into chunks.
- Stir in cooked linguine, chives and lemon zest into the pan, toss to coat evenly. Season with salt and black pepper to taste.

To plate
- Use a long-pronged fork to twist the pasta into a 'nest'. Carefully place the sliced lobster and serve it in the centre of a warm plate.

✪ CHEF'S TIP:
If you can't find lobster bisque, you can also try using other thick, creamy soups or sauces.

COD WITH SPICY *Chorizo*, BUTTER BEAN AND TOMATO STEW

Ingredients:

Cod & Brine
- 2 skinless cod fillet, 150g (5 oz) each
- 500ml (2 cups) of water
- 50g (1.8 oz) salt

Chorizo Stew
- 15ml (1 tbsp) olive oil
- 100g (3.5oz) chorizo, cut into cubes
- 1 red pepper, sliced thinly
- 200g (7 oz) canned butter beans
- 400g (14 oz) canned chopped tomatoes
- 50g (1.8 oz) pitted black olives
- 50g (1.8 oz) spinach leaves
- Salt and black pepper

This recipe is definitely a keeper, especially for the colder months - it's healthy comfort food. The spicy chorizo imparts volumes of flavor and depth to the tomato stew. It also goes brilliantly with the moist and smooth cod fillet (and a glass of Chenin Blanc). Serve it with crusty bread to mop up the remaining stew after you're done!

Method:

1 hour 30 minutes before
- Dissolve salt in a large bowl of water for a 10% brine. Brine the cod fillets in the liquid, refrigerated for 1 hour.

TIP: Cod can be replaced by other fish such as pollock, haddock, monkfish.

30 minutes before
- Set Codlo to preheat water bath to 52°C (125°F) with 20 minutes cooking time. Once target temperature is reached, remove fillets from brine. Seal them in a bag with some olive oil and submerge it in the water bath.

10 minutes before
- Sauté chorizo cubes and sliced pepper on medium heat for 3 minutes.
- Add in butter beans, chopped tomatoes and black olives. Simmer for another 3 minutes and season with salt and black pepper to taste. Add spinach last to wilt, remove from heat and set aside.

To plate
- Place a cod fillet on top of a bed of vegetables. Lightly season with black pepper. Serve immediately.

Ingredients:

Salmon & Brine
- 500ml (2 cups) water
- 50g (1.8oz) salt
- 2 skinless salmon fillet
- 30ml (1 tbsp) olive oil

Broccoli
- 4g (1 tsp) salt
- 200g (7 oz) broccoli

Parsley Sauce
- 10g (2 tsp) butter
- 10g (2 tsp) plain flour
- 150ml (0.6 cups) milk
- Salt & black pepper
- 0.5g (1/8 tsp) grated nutmeg
- 20g (0.7 oz) fresh parsley, chopped

Got a question?

Tweet us at @codlo - we'd love to hear from you!

S almon can be tricky to get right and is often overcooked. Try this sous-vide version for a smooth, velvety texture. For a really unique experience, remove the salmon skin and crisp them up separately for a great textural contrast with the buttery center. It's quick and easy to make too!

Method:

1 hour before
- Dissolve salt in a large bowl of water to prepare the brine. Brine the salmon fillets in the liquid, refrigerated for 20 minutes.
- Set Codlo to preheat water bath to 50°C (122°F) with 20 minutes cooking time.

15 minutes before
- Once target temperature is reached, remove fillets from brine. Seal them in a bag with some olive oil and submerge it in the water bath.
- Bring a large pot of salted water to boil. Blanch the broccoli florets for 2 minutes then shock them in cold water. Drain and set aside.
- For the sauce: dissolve butter in a pan on medium heat, mix in the flour thoroughly. Add milk gradually and stir well at each addition until smooth and thickened. Season the sauce with salt, black pepper and nutmeg. Add in parsley last. Set aside and keep warm.

To plate
- Pour some parsley sauce on each plate. Carefully place 1 salmon fillet on top. Serve with some broccoli.

○ CHEF'S TIP:

Brining helps prevent leaching of a white protein (albumin) from the salmon when cooked.

SESAME-CRUSTED *Tuna* TERIYAKI WITH CUCUMBER & CARROT RELISH

Given sushi's popularity, this is a great starter to have to wow your dinner party guests. The crunchy crust and the melt-in-your-mouth tuna will be unforgettable. You probably won't believe how easy and quick it is to make this!

I wished I had wider access to tuna - it took awhile to find good, quality cuts. Alternatively, this recipe works well with salmon too, cooked at a slightly higher temperature at 45°C (113°F), without the sesame crust. Just chill it immediately after cooking prior to slicing with a sharp knife. You'll get cleaner cuts that way, as salmon is velvety soft and fragile when warm.

Ingredients:

Tuna
- 2 tuna steaks

Relish
- 1 cucumber
- 1 carrot
- 10g (2 tsp) of sugar
- 5g (1 tsp) of salt

Teriyaki Sauce
- 50 ml (3 tbsp) light soy sauce
- 50 ml (3 tbsp) mirin
- 14g (1 tbsp) sugar

Sesame Crust
- 90g (3 oz) white sesame seeds
- 60g (2 oz) black sesame seeds
- 30ml (2 tbsp) sunflower oil

Method:

30 minutes before
- Set Codlo to preheat water bath to 43°C (109°F) with 15 minutes cooking time.
- Once target temperature is reached, seal the tuna in a bag and submerge it in the water bath.
- Peel long, wide strips of cucumber and carrots with a peeler. Place them in a bowl and toss with sugar and salt. Refrigerate until use.

10 minutes before
- Make the teriyaki sauce: bring soy sauce, mirin and sugar mixture to boil. Reduce heat to medium, simmer for 2 minutes until reduced. Remove from heat, set aside.
- Once the tuna is ready, carefully remove it from bag and pat dry with kitchen towels. Mix both the sesame seeds on a separate plate. Coat the tuna with sesame seeds on all sides. Heat up a pan with some oil on medium heat, gently toast the sesame-crusted tuna for 30 seconds a side until aromatic. Set aside.

To plate
- Slice the tuna against the grain into bite-size portions. Brush some teriyaki sauce in the middle of the plate at an angle. Arrange the tuna slices perpendicular to the sauce. Mold the carrot and cucumber relish into a tall tower with your hand and place it behind the tuna slices. Serve immediately with extra sauce on the side.

TIP: Cutting the cooked tuna requires some practice as it's fragile. Use a sharp knife and cut against the grain in one smooth motion.

⊙ CHEF'S TIP:

Tuna's great on the rarer side, so 47°C (117°F) is about as high as I'd go to enjoy it in its full glory.

BEEF

There's loads to learn about cooking beef sous-vide, but don't let that intimidate you. The complexity arises from whether a cut is tender or tough, thick or thin. As a rule of thumb, thinner and tender cuts require less cooking time than thicker and tougher ones. The sous-vide time and temperatures to all these permutations are covered in our handy Beef & Veal Temperature Chart in the following page, so no worries there!

To start, try the tender and/or thinner cuts and slowly progress to the larger roasts as you familiarize yourself with how time and temperature affects meat texture. For larger and/or tougher cuts that require longer cooking times, make sure you sear the surface of the meat beforehand and follow the recommended time and temperature settings. The recipes use many signature cuts that are remarkable when cooked sous-vide. But feel free to try out others too once you've cooked through these.

To start, try the tender and/or thinner cuts and slowly progress to the bigger roasts.

CODLO'S SOUS-VIDE *Guide* TO BEEF & VEAL

BEEF CUTS, EXPLAINED

(A) Tender and Thin   **(B)** Tender and Thick   **(C)** Tough and Thin   **(D)** Tough and Thick

Some of the best steak and roast cuts.
- **(A)** Rib Eye Steak
- **(B)** Rib Eye Roast
- **(D)** Short Ribs

The best cut for tenderness and flavour.
- **(B)** Tenderloin Roast
- **(A)** Tenderloin Steak (Filet Mignon)
- **(A)** Porterhouse Steak
- **(A)** T-Bone Steak
- **(A)** Top Loin Steak
- **(A)** Sirloin Steak

Plenty of connective tissue that melts during cooking.
- **(D)** Flat Iron
- **(D)** Pot Roast

Popular with soups, stews and deli cuts.
- **(D)** Brisket Point

Lean and very tough. Longer cooking times recommended.
- **(C)** Skirt Steak
- **(C)** Flank Steak

Regarded for its leanness, moderately tough.
- **(B)** Rump Roast
- **(A)** Rump Steak

(Cow diagram labels: CHUCK, BRISKET, RIB, PLATE, LOIN/SIRLOIN, ROUND)

COOKING IT RIGHT...

	🌡	Tender		Tough	
		(A) Thin 1.0-1.5 inches	**(B) Thick** 2-3 inches	**(C) Thin** 1-1.5 inches	**(D) Thick** 2-3 inches
Rare	50°C 122°F		Not Recommended		
Medium Rare	55°C 131°F		P 2.5-3 hours	P 4.5-6.5 hours		
Medium	60°C 140°F	1-2 hours	P 1.5-2 hours	P 2.5-4 hours	24 hours	36-72 hours
Done	70°C 158°F		P 1-1.5 hours	P 2-3 hours		

 Temperature   Timing   Time to pasteurize

RUMP STEAK WITH BABY LEAF & *Cherry* TOMATO SALAD

My brothers are big fans of steak. However, recipes often use vague cooking time estimates, when steak requires precise instructions depending on your cooker, beef cut and shape to get good results. Plenty of beautifully marbled cuts have gone overcooked, chewy and just plain wasted.

Sous-vide intensifies the flavor of beef and cooks it evenly throughout, so all you need to do at the end is sear it on high heat to char the outside for a nice, brown crust. It makes your steak results a lot more predictable and is quite a time saver, especially if you're cooking for a crowd!

Ingredients:

Steak
- 500g (1.1 lbs) rump steak, up to 3.8cm (1.5 inches) thick
- 30g (1 oz) butter

Gravy
- 10g (2 tsp) butter
- 10g (1.5 tbsp) plain flour
- 300ml (1.3 cups) beef stock

Vinaigrette
- 30ml (2 tbsp) olive oil
- 10ml (2 tsp) cider vinegar
- 5ml (1 tsp) of honey
- Salt and black pepper

Greens
- 80g (2.8 oz) mixed baby leaves
- 30g (1 oz) of cherry tomatoes, halved

Just want to say hi?
Give us a shout on Twitter @codlo!

Method:

1 hour 15 minutes before
- Set Codlo to preheat water bath to 53°C (127°F) with 1 hour cooking time.
- Once target temperature is reached, seal rump steak in a bag and submerge it in the water bath.

15 minutes before
- Once the steak is cooked, pat it dry with kitchen towels and sprinkle salt across its surface.
- Heat 30g butter in a heavy-based pan until hot. Sear the steak on high heat for just 20 seconds per side until brown. Remove and set aside.
- For the gravy: dissolve butter in a pan, add the flour and mix thoroughly. Add the stock in little increments and stir well at each addition until smooth. Season to taste and remove from heat. Strain the gravy, set aside.
- For the vinaigrette: combine olive oil, cider vinegar, honey, salt and black pepper in a bowl. Whisk thoroughly until emulsion is formed.
- Place salad leaves and cherry tomatoes in a large bowl. Drizzle with vinaigrette and gently mix to coat the leaves.

To plate
- Slice the steak across the grain and plate with dressed salad. Serve immediately with gravy.

✪ CHEF'S TIP:

Make sure your pan is really hot and salt the steak right before the quick sear. You'll get a nice brown crust without overcooking the perfectly pink center.

FRIED *Beef* NOODLES

Stir-fry is a fast and furious business, which can be annoying if you've slightly overcooked the meat slices due the high heat. For this version, I've cooked the beef sous-vide separately to get the best of both worlds - an extra smoky stir-fried noodles cooked on a well-seasoned wok, topped with extra juicy, medium-rare slices of beef.

Ingredients:

Beef Slices
- 500g (1.1 lbs) rump steak, up to 3.8cm (1.5 inches) thick

Fried Noodles
- 600g (20 oz) fresh egg noodles (blanched, drained)
- 45ml (3 tbsp) of oil
- 1 onion, sliced thinly
- 300g (10 oz) bean sprouts
- 5ml (1 tsp) dark soy sauce
- 15ml (1 tbsp) oyster sauce
- 15ml (1 tbsp) light soy sauce
- 1g (1/4 tsp) of sugar
- Black pepper
- 6 sprigs of spring onion, cut into strips

To Finish
- Sriracha chili sauce

Method:

1 hour 15 minutes before
- Set Codlo to preheat water bath to 53°C (127°F) with 1 hour cooking time. Once target temperature is reached, seal rump steak in a bag and submerge it in the water bath.

10 minutes before
- Heat oil in a wok and brown onions briefly. Add bean sprouts and stir-fry for a minute. Add the noodles and stir-fry over high heat for 30 seconds. Then add all seasonings and the stalks of spring onions. Cook for another 2 minutes. Stir in the leafy parts of spring onions last and fry for 1 minute. Set aside.
- Once the steak is cooked, pat it dry with kitchen towels and sprinkle salt across its surface.
- In a separate pan, heat 2 tbsp of oil until hot, sear the steak on high heat for 20 seconds each side until brown. Set aside and slice thinly against the grain.

To plate
- Place a portion of noodles in the center of the plate, topped with some sliced rump steak. Serve with chili sauce.

○ CHEF'S TIP:

For an awesome stir-fry, the wok needs to be hot and full attention is needed to stir constantly. So get your ingredients measured and ready on the side beforehand.

SKIRT *Steak* FAJITAS

Besides short ribs, skirt steak is also one of my new sous-vide discoveries, having taken greater interest in all cuts of beef.

I learned from my local butcher that skirt steak is popular among Mexican and Chinese restaurants, commonly used for fajitas and stir-fries as it's less expensive. Tough and lean, it requires a marinade to further tenderize and impart flavor.

Sous-vide really brings out the best in this steak fajita recipe. I really love Tex-Mex spice combinations and here it blends with the ultra tender rare beef to create a truly sumptous treat!

Ingredients:

Beef Fajita Strips
- 500g (1.1 lbs) skirt steak, up to 5cm (2 inches) thick
- 10g (2 tsp) butter
- Zest of 1 lime
- 3 strands of corianders, chopped
- 3 garlic gloves, minced
- 2g (1/2 tsp) cumin
- 2g (1/2 tsp) chili powder

Fajita Filling
- 30ml (2 tbsp) olive oil
- 3 bell peppers sliced
- 1 large onion, sliced
- Salt and pepper

For the Frying Pan
- 15ml (1 tbsp) olive oil
- 4g (1 tsp) salt

To Finish
- 8 flour tortillas
- Fresh coriander
- Sour cream
- Guacamole
- Salsa

Method:

2 days before
- Melt butter in a heavy based skillet. Sear the steak briefly on all sides for a total of 1 minute. Set aside to cool.
- For the marinade: add olive oil, zest, cumin, garlic, coriander and chili powder in a blender, process till smooth. Marinate the steak in the fridge for 4 hours or overnight.

1 day before
- Set Codlo to preheat water bath to 55°C (131°F) with 24 hours cooking time. Once target temperature is reached, remove steak from marinade. Seal steak in a bag and submerge it in the water bath.

10 minutes before
- Heat oil in a pan. Stir-fry peppers and onions for 5 minutes until softened. Season with salt and pepper.
- Once the steak is ready, remove it from the bag, pat dry and season both sides with salt. Heat 1 tbsp of oil on a heavy based skillet until hot. Sear the steak on high heat for 25 seconds per side. Slice the meat thinly against the grain.

To plate
- Place a few slices of steak in a warm flour tortilla with some sour cream, guacamole, coriander and salsa. Wrap and serve immediately.

Liked this one?
Tweet your favorites to @codlo!

✪ CHEF'S TIP:

Pre-searing not only helps kill off the surface bacteria on the meat, but also jump-starts the amazing flavor creation that develops over the long cooking time.

STEAK, SPINACH & *Farfalle* SALAD WITH PESTO DRESSING

Ingredients:

Steak
- 10g (2 tsp) butter
- 400g (14 oz) skirt steak

Pasta
- 350g (12 oz) farfalle,
- 30ml (2 tbsp) olive oil

Pesto & Salad
- 150g (5 oz) baby spinach
- 1 garlic clove, peeled
- 15ml (1 tbsp) olive oil
- 30g (1 oz) grated Parmesan
- 30g (1 oz) toasted pine nuts
- 5ml (1 tsp) fresh lemon juice
- Salt and pepper

This recipe can be prepared in advance and served cold. It's also great for using leftover sous-vide cooked meat that you've quick-chilled and refrigerated. It works as a starter or a main course and would definitely be the poshest work lunch ever!

Method:

1 day before
- Set Codlo to preheat water bath to 56°C (133°F) with 24 hours cooking time.
- Melt the butter in a pan. Sear the steak briefly for 20 seconds per side. Set aside. Once the target temperature is reached, seal the steak in a bag and submerge it in the water bath.

20 minutes before
- Cook the farfalle in a pot of boiling salted water until al dente. Drain and toss with 2 tbsp olive oil. Set aside to cool.
- For the pesto: combine 2/3 of the spinach, garlic, olive oil, Parmesan and pine nuts in a food processor. Pulse until smooth. Add the remaining 1/3 of the spinach and pulse briefly to roughly chop it. Season with salt, pepper and lemon juice to taste. Add pesto to the pasta and toss to coat, set aside.
- Once the steak is cooked, remove it from the bag. Pat dry with kitchen towels and season with salt. Heat 2 tbsp of oil in a pan until hot. Sear the steaks on high heat for 25 seconds per side. Slice meat thinly against the grain.

To plate
- Place a serving of pesto pasta in the middle of a plate, topped with generous portions of sliced skirt steak. Serve immediately.

SHORT RIBS *Tagliata*

I **love going shopping at my local butchers. Why? There often is plentiful supply of amazing but forgotten cuts, like short ribs.**

I'm used to preparing short ribs in thin slices, marinated then grilled, Korean BBQ-style, but I ventured into sous-vide short ribs after hearing of the rave reviews of the results.

Initially doubtful of the longer 2 days cooking time, I'm now convinced that this is how larger, tougher cuts should be treated - ultra low and slow. The longer cooking time is well justified - it allows the meat to remain medium rare throughout, while the low heat tenderizes and

slowly breaks down the collagen without losing too much moisture.

The result is just astounding and something that you'll understand only upon trying it yourself. Experiencing short ribs done this way will make you rethink your traditional prized beef cuts. If you prefer higher temperatures, here are some alternative settings that would work for a 5-7.6cm (2-3 inches) thick short rib:

- 62°C (142°F) for 36 hours
- 70°C (158°F) for 24 hours

Ingredients:

Beef Tagliata
- 600g (1.3 lbs) strip of boneless beef short ribs, 2.5-5cm (1-2 inches) thick

Dressing
- 45ml (3 tbsp) extra virgin olive oil
- 6g (1.5 tsp) dried, crushed chili flakes
- 8g (2 tsp) dried rosemary
- 15ml (1 tbsp) cider vinegar
- 2g (1/2 tsp) salt
- 5ml (1 tsp) lemon or lime juice

For the Frying Pan
- 15ml (1 tbsp) of olive oil
- Salt & black pepper

To Finish
- 250g (9 oz) cherry tomatoes, halved
- 80g (3 oz) wild rocket leaves
- 50g (1.8 oz) Parmesan, shaved

Method:

2 days before
- Set Codlo to preheat water bath to 56°C (133°F) with 48 hours cooking time.
- Heat a pan with oil until hot. Briefly sear all sides of the meat to brown in under 1 minute. Set aside. Once target temperature is reached, seal the short ribs in a bag and submerge in the water bath.

30 minutes before
- In a bowl, combine extra virgin olive oil, dried chili flakes, dried rosemary, cider vinegar, salt and lemon/lime juice to make the dressing.
- Once the short ribs are cooked, remove from bag and pat dry with kitchen towels. Season with salt and black pepper. Heat up a pan with oil until hot and briefly sear all sides of the meat to brown. Steep the meat in the bowl of dressing for 1 minute per side. Then, place meat on the chopping board and slice it thinly against the grain.
- Mix the cherry tomatoes in the dressing briefly, before adding in the wild rocket leaves. Gently toss to coat the salad evenly with the dressing. Adjust seasoning to taste.

To plate
- Place some wild rocket and cherry tomato salad in the center of the plates. Top it with some sliced short ribs and Parmesan shavings. Serve immediately.

○ CHEF'S TIP:

Pre-searing not only helps kill off the surface bacteria on the meat, but also jump-starts the amazing flavor creation that develops over the long cooking time.

LAMB

When buying lamb, just like other meat for sous-vide cooking, choose the leaner ones since you don't need the fat for it to taste amazing. Lamb's intense, rich and earthy flavor works not just with the usual mint sauce, but stronger aromatics like cumin and paprika too. With lamb, there is no need for a pre-searing step (unlike beef) for larger cuts as it tends to intensify the smell unnecessarily.

In this recipe series, we'll explore 4 cuts in particular: steak, rack, neck fillet and shanks, which serves as a solid introduction to cooking lamb sous-vide. Neck fillet and shanks are definitely are our firm favorites - they are super tender and unbelievably juicy after the low and slow treatment!

When buying lamb, just like other meat for sous-vide cooking, choose the leaner cuts.

CODLO'S SOUS-VIDE *Guide* TO LAMB

LAMB CUTS, EXPLAINED

Ⓐ Thin & Tender   **Ⓑ** Thick   **Ⓒ** Extra Thick

The 'jewel of the lamb', very tender and flavorful.
Ⓐ Sirloin Chop
Ⓑ Loin Chop
Ⓐ Loin Roast

One of the tougher cuts, generally sold for stews or grinding. It also is perfect for low and slow cooking!
Ⓐ Neck Chop
Ⓑ Neck Fillet Roast

Flavorsome and nutritious, a prime cut with very little fat. A lamb shank is the bottom cut of the leg.
Ⓒ Shank
Ⓒ Leg of Lamb
Ⓐ Chump

Often sold as two separate joints, blade and arm (knuckle). Besides cooked whole, shoulder can also be trimmed, cubed and cooked in casseroles or curries.
Ⓒ Shoulder Roast
Ⓐ Arm Chop
Ⓐ Blade Chop

The rack of lamb is a tender, flavorsome and highly prized cut. The breast is cheaper but highly versatile.
Ⓑ Rolled Shank Roast   Ⓐ Rack of Lamb

TREAT YOUR LAMB RIGHT...

	🌡		**Tender**		**Tough**	
		Ⓐ	**Thin** (1-1.5 inches)	**Ⓑ** **Thick** (1.5-2.5 inches)	**Ⓒ** **Extra Thick** (up to 3 inches)	
Medium Rare	55°C 131°F	1 hour	🅟 2.5-3.5 hours			
Medium	60°C 140°F	1 hour	🅟 1.5-2 hours	🅟 8-24 hours	🅟 24-48 hours	
Done	70°C 158°F	1 hour	🅟 1-1.5 hours			

Temperature

Timing

Time to pasteurize

RACK OF LAMB WITH *Roasted* VEGETABLES & RED WINE SAUCE

R ack of lamb is one of those things that can be served in a formal style in an individual dish, or more family-style for Sunday roast where everyone just grabs one like a lollipop.

What I love about this dish is how the welcoming color, aroma and flavor of the roasted vegetables worked as a nice change to the usual mash. Paired with a perfectly pink lamb and a zesty red wine sauce, all you need is a great glass of red for a perfect Sunday afternoon.

Ingredients:

Lamb
- 500g (1.1 lbs) rack of lamb, trimmed
- Fresh thyme sprigs
- Black pepper

Roast Vegetables
- 1 potato, cut into chunks
- 1 carrot, cut into chunks
- 9 asparagus spears
- 3 garlic cloves, crushed
- 1 red onion, quartered
- Olive oil
- Salt & black pepper
- Fennel seeds

Red Wine Sauce
- 4 shallots, quartered
- 150ml (0.6 cups) beef stock
- 150ml (0.6 cups) dry red wine
- 60ml (4 tbsp) balsamic vinegar

Enjoyed this?
Tweet your favorites to @codlo!

Method:

1 hour 15 minutes before
- Set Codlo to preheat water bath to 57°C (135°F) with 1 hour cooking time.
- Season the lamb with thyme and black pepper. Wrap the bones with aluminum foil - this prevents the bones from puncturing your bag in the water bath. Once target temperature is reached, seal the lamb in a bag and submerge it in the water bath.
- Parboil the potatoes and carrots in a large pot for 7 minutes. In the last minute, add in the asparagus to blanch briefly. Drain the vegetables and leave to dry.

45 minutes before
- Preheat oven to 190°C (374°F). Toss the potatoes, carrots, asparagus, purple onion and garlic cloves with some olive oil. Season with salt, black pepper and fennel seeds. Roast the vegetables for 40 minutes. Set aside.

10 minutes before
- Once the lamb is ready, remove from bag and pat dry with kitchen towel. Heat a skillet without oil. Season lamb with salt, sear it skin-side down on medium high heat until golden (5-6 min). Turn over and cook for 30 second. Set aside.
- For the sauce: pour out most of the fat of the same skillet. Add shallots to brown. Then, add balsamic vinegar, wine and stock to reduce until half. Adjust seasoning to taste. Strain sauce and set aside.

TIP: Be careful here as the hot fat renders out, quite a lot of sizzling and popping going on!

To plate
- Cut lamb into portions along the rib bone. Serve with roasted vegetables and red wine sauce.

LAMB *Steak* WITH BUTTERNUT SQUASH MASH

Ingredients:

Lamb
- 4 boneless lamb steaks,
- each 2.5-3.8 cm (1-1.5 inches) thick

Butternut Squash Mash
- 1kg (2.2 lbs) butternut squash, sliced
- lengthwise, seeds removed
- 15g (1 tbsp) butter
- 50ml (3 tbs) of milk
- Salt & black pepper

Accompaniments
- 8 asparagus spears, washed and trimmed

Gravy
- 10g (2 tsp) butter
- 10g (1.5 tbsp) plain flour
- 300ml (1.3 cups) lamb stock

For the Frying Pan
- Salt
- 30g (1 tbsp) butter

○ CHEF'S TIP:

The thin steaks are deliberately cooked on the rare side so there's more leeway when browning the crust later on to minimize overcooking.

A vailable all year round, popular lamb cuts tend to be the leg, shoulder, rack and loin, which are great for roasts.

But you can enjoy lamb on smaller scale too and even have time to make one like this during weekdays. Lean and flavorful, lamb steaks paired with a little butternut squash and gravy makes for simple comfort food.

Method:

1 hour 15 minutes before
- Set Codlo to preheat water bath to 55°C (131°F) with 1 hour cooking time.
- Once target temperature is reached, seal the steaks in a bag and submerge them in the water bath.

25 minutes before
- Place both halves of the squash, cut side down in a large skillet. Add boiling water up to halfway. Place the lid, cook for 25 minutes on medium heat.
- Remove squash carefully, scoop out the flesh with a spoon. Add butter, milk, salt and black pepper, to taste. Mash the squash until smooth, set aside.

15 minutes before
- Blanch the asparagus for 2 minutes, shock them in ice-cold water, drain and set aside.
- For the gravy: dissolve butter in the pan, add in flour and mix thoroughly. Add the stock gradually and stir well at each addition until smooth. Strain, set aside.
- Once lamb steaks are ready, pat them dry with kitchen towels and lightly season with salt. Melt butter in a pan until hot, sear the steaks on high heat for 20 seconds each side. Set aside.

To plate
- Spoon mash slightly off-center on a plate. Carefully place a piece of lamb steak on top of the mash, topped with an asparagus. Drizzle a spoonful of gravy and serve immediately.

MOROCCAN *Lamb* SHANK WITH COUS COUS

am a big fan of Moroccan food - rich, earthy and flavorful. Many Moroccan dishes rely on slow braising and long cooking times - a prime candidate for sous-vide! I've had superb lamb shanks before - tender, but just missing that extra juiciness. With sous-vide, now you can have fall-off-the-bone tender lamb that's still pink and moist!

Ingredients:

Lamb & Marinade
- 2 lamb shanks
- 4g (1 tsp) paprika
- 2g (1/2 tsp) each: dried chili flakes, ground coriander, cumin, cinnamon and turmeric

Stew
- 30ml (2 tbsp) olive oil
- 1 yellow onion, chopped
- 2 garlic cloves
- 20g (0.7 oz) ginger, skinned
- 175ml (3/4 cups) of chicken stock
- 400g (14 oz) canned chopped tomatoes
- 5ml (1 tsp) lemon juice
- 10ml (2 tsp) honey
- Salt and black pepper

To Finish
- Couscous, cooked
- Dried fruits
- Almond or pistachio
- Coriander, chopped

Method:

3 days before
- Mix paprika, chili flakes, ground coriander, cumin, cinnamon and turmeric together and rub them onto the lamb shanks. Refrigerate to marinate overnight.

2 days before
- Set Codlo to preheat water bath to 60°C (140°F) with 48 hours cooking time. Once target temperature is reached, seal the lamb in a bag and submerge it in the water bath.

TIP: Before sealing the lamb, cover all protruding bones with aluminum foil to prevent your bag from being punctured.

15 minutes before
- Once lamb shank is ready, remove from bag and pat dry with kitchen towel. Heat up olive oil in a pan and brown all sides of the lamb briefly for 1 minute. Remove and set aside.
- Mince onion, garlic and ginger in a blender until fine. Add this mixture to the same pan to brown until fragrant.
- Gradually pour in the stock and stir in the chopped tomatoes, lemon juice and honey. Reduce heat to low and add in lamb shanks to simmer for 2 minutes. Season to taste and remove from heat.

To plate
- Mix couscous with chopped dried fruits or nuts, divide equally among plates. Serve with a lamb shank and sauce on the side, topped with chopped coriander.

Got a question?
Let us know on Twitter via @codlo!

☺ CHEF'S TIP:
Given the uneven shape of the shanks, you can use a blowtorch instead of browning it in a pan.

LAMB & *Spinach* CURRY

L amb neck is a hidden gem, brought to life by slow cooking. It's a tougher, forgotten cut, yet inexpensive and super tender if done right. Both Xi and I are hardcore British Indian curry fans - some even say we drink curry - and we're always floored by how this cut of lamb transforms under the sous-vide treatment.

Ingredients:

Lamb Neck & Rub
- 12g (1 tbsp) each: ground cumin and coriander
- 4g (1 tsp) each: ground turmeric and chili powder
- 600g (1.3 lbs) boneless lamb neck fillet, trimmed
- 15ml (1 tbsp) vegetable oil

For the Frying Pan
- 45ml (3 tbsp) vegetable oil

Spinach Curry
- 2 onions, chopped
- 10 garlic cloves, chopped
- 1 green chili, sliced
- 20g (0.7 oz) ginger, peeled and chopped
- 400g (14 oz) canned chopped tomatoes
- 80g (2.8 oz) spinach leaves
- 30g (2 tbsp) plain yoghurt
- 4g (1 tsp) garam masala
- Salt and black pepper

To Finish
- Coriander, finely chopped
- Naan breads

Method:

2 days before
- Mix spices together in a large bowl, set half aside for later use. Use the remaining half of it to rub onto the lamb neck fillets. Refrigerate to marinate overnight.

1 day before
- Set Codlo to preheat water bath to 57°C (135°F) with 24 hours cooking time. Once target temperature is reached, seal the neck fillets in a bag with some vegetable oil and submerge the bag in the water bath.

30 minutes before
- Heat oil in a pan. Remove cooked neck fillets from the bag and pat dry with kitchen towel. Briefly sear all sides of the lamb for 1 minute until fragrant. Remove meat from heat. Set aside to cool before dicing into large cubes.
- Meanwhile, pulse onion, garlic, ginger and green chili in a blender until it forms a smooth paste. Add the paste to the same pan to brown until fragrant for 15 minutes. Stir in the chopped tomatoes and reduce to heat to medium low to simmer for another 5 minutes.
- Remove pan from heat and add in the spinach and lamb pieces. Stir to incorporate until spinach wilts. Then add some yoghurt and garam masala. Season to taste with salt and black pepper.

TIPS: Make sure you sauté the aromatics until brown and caramelized, before adding spices. This curry is mild: use 2 green chilies if you like it hotter. Add more yoghurt if it's too spicy!

To plate
- Serve curry immediately with some basmati rice, naan bread or chapatti, sprinkled with some coriander.

VEGETABLES

8**4°C (183°F) is your magic number for most vegetables, fruits and legumes. This is because they contain pectin - the molecular 'glue' that holds the cells together - that only starts to break down at 84°C (183°F). Sous-vide cooked vegetables, fruits and legumes are tender yet retain their bite (no more mushiness), with a stronger, sweeter and more concentrated natural flavor as it cooks in its own juice.**

Two things to note though: do take extra care when dealing with higher temperatures for vegetables - they'll scald this time, unlike the usual 55°C (131°F) range! Also, here's where having a chamber vacuum sealer may help in effecting a proper seal (since certain odd shapes of vegetables or fruit may make it trickier to remove air) as well as trying out new techniques such as compression and quick-pickling.

We cover the basics here in our recipes which would work using the water displacement method (without vacuum sealers) - please refer to the Techniques & Equipment section for further instructions.

CODLO'S SOUS-VIDE *Guide* TO VEGETABLES

COOK YOUR GREENS RIGHT

ROOT VEGETABLES

Beet, carrot, potato, turnip, yam, daikon (Japanese radish), radish, parsnip, celeriac, sweet potato, water chestnut, artichoke

84°C (183°F)
1-4 hours

NOTES:
Up to 1 inch thick. Chop, dice or split them as needed.

OTHER VEGETABLES

Corn, eggplant (aubergine), fennel, onions, squashes

84°C (183°F)
45 min-2 hours

NOTES:
Up to 1 inch thick. Chop, dice or split them as needed.

LEGUMES

Beans (borlotti, navy, black, butter, azuki, pinto etc)

84°C (183°F)
6-24 hours

NOTES:
Pre-soak beans for 6-8 hours beforehand. Cook with sufficient liquid (water or stock) in the bag as the beans will absorb them.

Chick peas

84°C (183°F)
6-9 hours

NOTES:
Pre-soak required, then add flavoring (herbs, oil, salt) in bag before cooking.

Lentils

84°C (183°F)
1-3 hours

NOTES:
Pre-soak required, then add flavoring (herbs, oil, salt) in bag before cooking.

FRUIT

Melons, apple, pear, mango, peach, nectarine, blueberry, strawberry, plum.

84°C (183°F) for
45 min - 90 min

NOTES:
Amazing cooked with flavored syrups, juice, tea, vinegar etc.

Rhubarb (tender stem)

60°C (140°F) for
30 min - 1 hour

Great with flavored syrups (vanilla especially).

DID YOU KNOW?

The tomato is botanically a fruit, but was declared a vegetable by the US Supreme Court in 1893.

Eating garlic can keeps mosquitoes away - not just vampires!

Red and yellow bell peppers have four times as much vitamin C as oranges.

SWEET POTATO, *Beetroot* AND FETA SALAD

This colorful salad packs a (nutritious) punch! Sous-vide cooked beetroot and sweet potatoes are firm and naturally sweet. They are amazing on their own without the need for much seasoning. Lightly tossed in simple honey mustard dressing, sprinkled with feta cheese and pumpkin seeds, the salad transforms into something magical - sweet and savory with a hint of spiciness, occasionally surprising you with crunchiness.

Ingredients:

Beetroot & Sweet Potato
- 450g (1 lbs) sweet potato, cut into cubes
- Salt and black pepper
- 15g (1 tbsp) butter
- 2 raw beetroot, skinned and cut into cubes
- 15g (1 tbsp) butter

Couscous
- 50g (1.8 oz) instant couscous
- 2.5ml (1/2 tsp) garlic oil

Salad Dressing
- 30ml (2 tbsp) olive oil
- 15ml (1 tbsp) honey
- 15ml (1 tbsp) cider vinegar
- 5ml (1 tsp) Dijon mustard

To Finish
- 80g (2.8 oz) spinach leaves
- 1 red chili, deseeded, chopped
- Freshly ground black pepper
- 30g (1 oz) roasted pumpkin seeds
- 120g (4.2 oz) feta cheese, crumbled

Method:

1 hour 10 minutes before
- Set Codlo to preheat water bath to 84°C (183°F) with 1 hour cooking time. Place the sweet potato and beetroot pieces in 2 separate bags along with salt, black pepper and butter.
- Once target temperature is reached, seal and submerge both the bags in the water bath.

10 minutes before
- Place couscous and garlic oil in a bowl and pour 50ml of boiling water on it. Stir to mix evenly and set it aside to sit for 10 minutes.
- To make the dressing, place olive oil, honey, cider vinegar and Dijon mustard in a bowl and whisk until combined.
- Remove cooked beets and sweet potato from pouches and pat them dry with kitchen towels.

To plate
- To finish, place spinach leaves, chili, sweet potato, beetroot and couscous in a large mixing bowl. Pour over the dressing and lightly toss to coat evenly. Season with black pepper.
- Divide salad onto individual plates, topped with some feta cheese and pumpkin seeds prior to serving.

TIPS: Goat's cheese is a great substitute for feta. If you don't have pumpkin seeds at hand, try chopped nuts instead.

○ CHEF'S TIP:
Although cooked at the same temperature, do use a separate bag for the beets so that the color won't stain the bright orange sweet potatoes!

EGGPLANT *Parmigiana*

Eggplant (or aubergine) is delicious and comes in a variety of shapes and sizes, not to mention various shades of purple too. It makes a perfect canvas to which aromatic herbs and spices can be added - and it soaks them all up nicely so you can be really creative with eggplants! This classic recipe gets updated with sous-vide so you'll still get the same cheesy crust but with firmer, non-mushy nor greasy eggplant.

Ingredients:

Eggplants
- 700g (1.5 lbs) eggplants, sliced crosswise about 1/4 inch (5mm) thick
- Salt and black pepper
- Olive oil

Parmagiana Sauce
- 15ml (1 tbsp) olive oil
- 3 garlic cloves, minced
- 1 onion, diced
- 2 x 400g (14oz) canned chopped tomatoes
- 100g (3.5 oz) mushroom, sliced
- 1g (1/4 tsp) dried oregano
- 1g (1/4 tsp) dried basil
- Salt and black pepper

To Finish
- 200g (7 oz) mozzarella, shredded
- 100g (3.5 oz) Parmesan, grated

Need more tips?
Give us a shout on Twitter @codlo!

Method:

1 hour before
- Set Codlo to preheat water bath to 84°C (183°F) with 45 minutes cooking time. Sprinkle each side of the sliced eggplant with salt and pepper and place them in one layer in a bag with 1 tbsp of olive oil each.
- Once target temperature is reached, seal and submerge the bags in the water bath.

30 minutes before
- Heat olive oil in a pan on medium heat. Add the garlic and onions to brown for 3 minutes. Stir in mushrooms and chopped tomatoes, bring it to a gentle simmer for 15 minutes until reduced. Add in dried oregano and basil. Adjust seasoning to taste. Remove from heat.
- Preheat oven to 200°C (392°F). Rapidly chill the bags containing eggplant slices in ice-cold water.
- Meanwhile, lightly grease a baking dish and spread a thin layer of tomato sauce at its base. Cover with a layer of eggplant and mozzarella. Repeat this order of layers, ending with a layer of sauce and a generous final sprinkle of Parmesan. Bake for 12 minutes until bubbling and browned.

TIP: We used a 25cm x 18cm (10" x 7") rectangular baking dish for this recipe.

To plate
- Let the baking dish cool slightly prior to serving. Cut into large squares and serve.

○ CHEF'S TIP:

Exposed eggplant slices will oxidize and turn brown quickly, so slice them right before cooking. If you have to leave cut slices out, plunging them in water and lemon juice will help keep them fresh.

BLACK BEAN & CORN *Quesadilla* WITH CHUNKY GUACAMOLE

Everyone loves quesadilla - you can have endless filling variations to suit tastes and preferences. It's the ideal dinner party nibble to have as you can keep churning freshly toasted ones out as the fillings are cooked and prepared in advance. But it's what you do to the fillings that matter. Imagine being able to subtly infuse the beans with any flavor (for me, it's gotta be garlic!) and make the world's sweetest, crunchiest corn with just a teaspoon of butter. Try it and see, corn will never taste the same again.

Ingredients:

Black Beans
- 1 liter (4 cups) water
- 310g (11oz) dried black beans
- 600ml (2.5 cups) water
- 4g (1 tsp) salt

Corn
- 1 ear of corn, shucked
- 4g (1 tsp) butter
- 2g (1/2 tsp) salt

Chunky Guacamole
- 2 avocados, diced
- 1 red onion, diced
- 1 tomato, diced
- 30ml (2 tbs) lime juice
- 10g (0.4 oz) coriander leaves

Bean & Corn Mix
- Salt and black pepper
- 6g (1.5 tsp) chili powder
- 4g (1 tsp) paprika
- 2g (1/2 tsp) each: cumin, salt and black pepper

To Finish
- 8 flour tortillas
- 80g (3 oz) cheddar cheese, shredded

Method:

1 day before
- Pre-soak dried beans with 4 cups of water in the refrigerator overnight.

6 hours before
- Set Codlo to preheat water bath to 84°C (183°F) with 6 hours cooking time.
- Once target temperature is reached, drain the beans, seal them in a bag with water and salt and submerge it in the water bath.

1 hour before
- Seal corn kernels, butter and salt in a bag and submerge it in the water bath.

20 minutes before
- Place 1 avocado, red onion, tomato, coriander leaves and lime juice into a blender. Pulse until fine, remove and serve in a bowl. Mix in the remaining diced avocado. Season with salt and pepper to taste.
- Drain the cooked corn and beans. Place the beans in a large bowl and mash some of them for a chunky texture. Then, add in chili powder, paprika, cumin, salt, black pepper, corn and mix until well combined. Adjust seasoning to taste.
- Lightly grease a pan and place it on medium heat. Place a flour tortilla on the pan. Spread 3 tablespoons of the bean mixture and some cheddar cheese on one half of each tortilla.
- Reduce heat to low, allow cheese to melt slightly, before folding over the tortilla in half. Once the tortilla is nice and brown, remove it from the pan. Repeat with the remaining tortilla, cheese and bean mixture.

TIP: Stop guacamole from browning by adding a thin layer of water on top and refrigerating. Just pour the water off prior to serving. Alternatively you can press cling film onto the top of your guacamole. The key here is to prevent air from getting to it!

To plate
- Slice each quesadilla into 2 pieces and serve with guacamole.

Japanese VEGETABLE CURRY

There's this katsu curry institution in London we visited frequently as students because they had the crispiest, largest portion of katsu curry ever, for just £6 ($9). When I first visited Tokyo, we discovered something even better - amazing Japanese curry places that let you pick your preferred curry heat level! Here's how to make your own Japanese curry from scratch, with a touch of sous-vide, of course.

Ingredients:

Carrot & Potatoes
- 1 carrot, cut into chunks
- 1 potato, cut into chunks
- Butter
- Salt and black pepper

Curry Roux
- Vegetable oil
- 2 onion, sliced
- 30ml (2 tbsp) sunflower oil
- 20g (3 tbsp) flour
- 18g (1.5 tbsp) garam masala
- 4g (1 tsp) chili powder
- 2g (1/2 tsp) sugar
- 7g (1/2 tbsp) each: ground cumin, coriander and turmeric
- 1g (1/4 tsp) each: chili flakes, mustard seeds and ground ginger

To Finish
- 750ml (3 cups) vegetable stock
- 2 apples, skinned and grated
- 2g (1/2 tsp) garam masala
- Salt and black pepper
- 300g (10 oz) firm tofu, cubed
- 50g (1.8 oz) spinach leaves

Method:

1 hour 10 minutes before
- Set Codlo to preheat water bath to 84°C (183°F) with 1 hour cooking time.
- Once target temperature is reached, seal carrot and potatoes in separate bags with 1 tsp of butter (each), salt and black pepper. Submerge the bags in the water bath.

20 minutes before
- Heat oil in a saucepan over medium heat. Sauté the onion until brown and caramelized for 15 minutes.
- Meanwhile, make the curry roux: heat sunflower oil over low heat in a separate saucepan. Add in flour, stir vigorously for 6 minutes until you have a thick, dark paste. Stir in the garam masala, sugar, chili powder and the rest of the spices until it starts to be a little crumbly. Remove from heat and set aside.

TIP: Make sure that you cook the roux on low heat with constant stirring to ensure that it browns evenly without burning.

5 minutes before
- Once the onions are caramelized, add in stock, grated apple, garam masala and salt. Simmer for 2 minutes before reducing heat to low.
- Stir in the cooked potatoes, carrots along with the bag juices. Add in the curry roux, stir until sauce is thick and lump-free, before adding tofu and spinach. Remove from heat and set aside. Adjust seasoning to taste.

To plate
- Serve vegetable curry with Japanese short grain rice.

☻ CHEF'S TIP:
This curry goes just as well with seafood, chicken, beef or pork too.

TECHNIQUES AND *Equipment*

In short, it depends.

A vacuum sealer isn't necessary if you cook for immediate serving ("cook-serve"). Good quality, resealable, food-grade plastic bags with the water displacement method works well for home use.

A vacuum sealer is recommended if you intend to store sous-vide cooked food for a *prolonged* time for consumption later (long term "cook-chill"), or use advanced techniques such as food compression and flash-pickling (which requires a chamber vacuum). We recommend exploring these at a later stage once you become more familiar with the cook-serve method.

The purpose of minimizing air in the bag is to ensure an efficient heat distribution from the water bath to the food for even cooking, as air is a poor conductor of heat. This is also the reason why you can survive in a sauna at 70°C (158°F), but scald your fingers if they are dipped in a water bath for a few seconds at the same temperature.

Although bulky and expensive, **chamber vacuum sealers** are very effective at making bags vacuum-sealed. Given the large chamber, multiple bags can be vacuum-sealed at once and liquid marinades in the bag would stay put. Its ability to pull a strong vacuum enables other advanced techniques such as food compression and flash-pickling. These are generally used under professional settings.

On the other end of the spectrum are the compact **hand-held vacuum sealers** that work with special resealable bags with a valve. Hand-held units are affordable but the strength of vacuum is weaker and quality varies by manufacturer. It may be tricky to seal food with liquid, but this is easily solvable by freezing the liquid marinade in ice cube trays beforehand.

Clamp-style vacuum sealers are also relatively compact but operate using heat sealing of pouches (without a zip seal or valve). Similar to hand-helds, sealing food with liquid is tricky but you can freeze the liquid marinade beforehand.

With sous-vide cooking, vacuum sealers are optional for most cases, unless you require prolonged storage of food cooked sous-vide. This is explained in more detail in the previous section.

A simple water displacement method works for sous-vide cooking - you'll master this with just a bit of practice. It's best to start with a large bowl of cold water to do this.

Here's how you do it:

1. Place ingredient (in this case, duck breast) into a food-safe resealable freezer bag.

2. Seal the lip of the bag, leaving a small hole unsealed at the end.

3. Press to flatten food evenly and push out most of the air.

4. Submerge bag in a large bowl of water until it reaches just below the zip closure. The water pushes out most of the air in the bag.

5. Seal the bag completely.

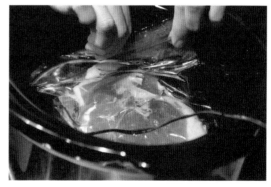

BRINING

At its simplest, brining is the act of soaking meat in a solution of water and salt, while refrigerated. **Brining makes leaner cuts of meat (such as pork, fish and poultry) juicier** as some of the brine solution is absorbed into the meat, but more importantly it improves moisture retention when cooking.

Composition of brines vary widely. They are typically a 5%-10% salt solution (50g-100g salt per liter of water), but you can be quite creative here by adding other flavorings (e.g. sugar, herbs and aromatics) which you'd like to impart to the meat. If adding complex flavorings, make sure the brine is heated beforehand to 'activate' the spices and seasonings better. But only add the meat in once the brine is cool!

The length of brining time depends on the type and size of meat. Delicate seafood like shrimps or fish takes 20 - 30 minutes, slices of poultry or pork is perfect brined for 2-3 hours, whereas larger cuts such as pork shoulder or beef brisket can be brined up to 2 days.

Brining is easy and economical: all you need is salt, water, a large bowl and a refrigerator.

1. Once the salt (and other flavorings, if added) is dissolved and the brine is cooled to room temperature, add in the meat to the brine.

2. Make sure the meat is completely submerged in the brine. Cover with cling film and refrigerate until use.

SOUS-VIDE *Food* SAFETY

Sous-vide is just another method of cooking, so most of the hygiene and safety know-how is not new. However, given the lower temperatures used, there are a few need-to-knows on:

- Time and temperature
- Pasteurization
- Food hygiene
- Food storage

THE IMPORTANCE OF TIME AND TEMPERATURE IN SOUS-VIDE COOKING

A common misconception about low temperature cooking is that it is unsafe as it involves cooking in lower temperatures that are in the bacterial "danger zone" of 5°C-55°C (41°F-131°F).

Food safety is a function of both time and temperature; a low cooking temperature would be perfectly safe if maintained at that temperature for long enough to achieve pasteurization.

Pasteurization isn't strictly necessary for safe consumption (think sushi!), however it's a requirement if cook-chill is needed. As a reminder, there are 2 types of low-temperature cooking: cook-serve and cook-chill. With cook-serve, food is cooked and served immediately; whereas cook-chill means that food is cooked, chilled, stored and reheated prior to consumption at a later date.

Generally, food items that are heated and served within 4 hours are considered safe (including unpasteurized food), but meat that is cooked for longer to tenderize must reach a temperature of at least 55°C (131°F) within 4 hours and then be kept there, in order to pasteurize the meat.

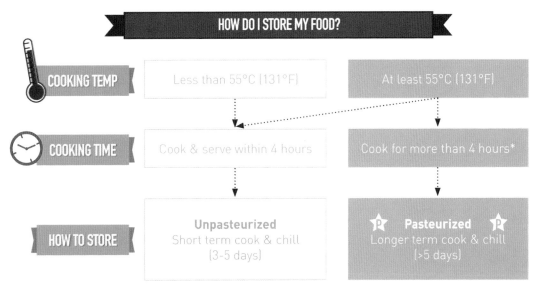

HOW DO I STORE MY FOOD?

COOKING TEMP	Less than 55°C (131°F)	At least 55°C (131°F)
COOKING TIME	Cook & serve within 4 hours	Cook for more than 4 hours*
HOW TO STORE	**Unpasteurized** Short term cook & chill (3-5 days)	**P Pasteurized P** Longer term cook & chill (>5 days)

This rule generally applies for meat cuts up to 2 inches thick. For accurate details on pasteurization times, please refer to each respective food section's Codlo Guide (also see next page).

THE CONCEPT OF PASTEURIZATION

Unpasteurized food is considered raw or minimally cooked and not suitable for highly susceptible, pregnant or those with weaker immune systems ("immuno-compromised").

That said, **unpasteurized food is safe to eat with practice of good food hygiene** and using fresh, high quality ingredients - or else we wouldn't have sushi, rare steak or carpaccio!

Pasteurizing food cooked sous-vide requires a minimum cooking temperature of 55°C (131°F). You can see pasteurization times and temperatures in each food section's Codlo Guide page.

PAGE 25

PAGE 33

PAGE 53

PAGE 67

PAGE 79

PAGE 91

Sous-vide cooking is safe with good food hygiene practices, purchase of fresh food and adherence to the time-temperature guidelines. These precautions apply to conventional cooking methods as well!

Key food hygiene best practices

1. Buy fresh, good quality ingredients that are thoroughly cleaned.
2. Keep ingredients refrigerated (or frozen) at less than 5°C (41°F) until use.
3. Don't let food be in the bacteria "danger zone" of 5°C-55°C (41°F-131°F) for more than 4 hours.
4. Minimize cross contamination by using separate cutting boards and storage units for different food, such as vegetables, fruits, fish, poultry and meat.
5. Serve freshly cooked food right away or follow proper chilling and storage practices (see next section).

FOOD STORAGE Q&A

Can I pre-prepare raw food, seal and freeze it and cook them from frozen later?

Yes, you'll need to add additional cooking time for the food item to thaw in the water bath. The speed of thawing depends on the item's thickness, shape and cooking temperature. It could range from an additional 30 minutes (for 2.5cm / 1 inch thickness) up to double the minimum cooking time of recipes.

For prolonged freezer storage (more than 5 days), do make sure you seal it properly with a vacuum sealer to avoid freezer burn. Avoid adding salt if you're seasoning raw ingredients prior to sealing and freezing as it tends to create a 'cured,' firmer texture that's less juicy when cooked.

What's the difference between shorter and longer term cook-chill?

Cook-chill means that ingredients are cooked, chilled, stored and reheated later. The length referred to here is the storage time. Generally, we'd define "longer term" as storing more than 5 days. The method of storage (refrigeration vs. freezing and usage of vacuum sealer) is affected by the desired storage time and pasteurization, although all cook-chill processes involve a rapid chilling (or quick chill) process prior to storage.

How do you quick chill sous-vide cooked foods?

The goal for rapid chilling is to minimize the time of cooked food staying within the bacteria "danger zone" temperature range of 5°C-55°C (41°F-131°F). It also prevents moisture from forming in the bag - and hence ice crystals - which may affect storage quality.

To do this: once the pouches have finished cooking, completely submerge them - still sealed - in an ice bath containing equal amounts of ice cubes and water for about 1 hour. Then, remove the pouches from the ice bath, dry them prior to refrigeration (for a few days) or freezer storage (for a few months). If you notice that the pouches are no longer airtight, it's best to repackage the cooked items in a new bag and make it airtight again prior to storage.

Note that storage temperature is critical: in general it should always be at most 5°C (41°F) (which is good for 3-5 days refrigeration), but colder is better for prolonged storage.

It's advisable to label the pouches with the date and time of storage (so you don't forget). It's also good practice to portion your servings in separate bags for easy reheating later.

How long can sous-vide cooked food be kept in the fridge for safe consumption?

With a proper quick-chill and storage process:

- Unpasteurized food should be consumed within 3-5 days. We'd recommend a maximum of 3 days for delicate food items like seafood.
- Pasteurized food should be consumed within 7-10 days.

How long can sous-vide cooked food be kept in the freezer for safe consumption?

If using resealable bags like heavy-duty Ziploc pouches, generally it's good for a few days (say 3-5 days) in the freezer. For longer storage times, it's best to use thicker vacuum packaging bags and seal it airtight prior to freezing, which would last 3-6 months. This is because the thinner layers of resealable bags would allow gases to exchange over time between inside and outside of the bag.

Can I reheat sous-vide cooked items from the fridge or freezer?

To reheat, all you need to do is submerge previously sealed food pouches (straight from fridge or freezer) into the water bath at the target serving temperature (never higher than the original cooking temperature). The amount of time needed depends on the speed of the food reaching this temperature throughout. As a general guide, for food items up to 2.5cm-3.8cm thick (1-1.5 inches), it takes about 30 minutes (from the fridge) to 1 hour (from frozen).

SAFETY OF USING *Plastics* IN SOUS-VIDE COOKING

The main concern about cooking in plastic bags involve leaching of potentially harmful chemicals, such as BPA (bisphenol-A) and phthalates from the bag into the food. Food grade plastic bags, certified as suitable for cooking by their manufacturer, are safe to use.

Not all plastics are suitable for sous-vide. Avoid the ones containing polyvinyl chloride (PVC) as they contain plasticizers. Suitable ones are bags made from high-density polyethylene (HDPE) or low-density polyethylene (LDPE) - most sous-vide or food-safe freezer bags fit this criteria.

In relation to resealable bags such as Ziploc, sous-vide practitioners often go for the heavy-duty ones suitable for freezer storage. They are BPA-free and often used for sous-vide when prolonged storage is not needed. We leave it to experts to comment on this issue:

Harold McGee, author and prominent food science expert commented in an article in New York Times (11 August 2008):

> "Heavy-duty Ziploc bags are made from polyethylene (PE) and are approved for contact with hot foods. True sous-vide cooking involves vacuum-packing the food, which zipping a bag won't do for you. But you can certainly use the bag to immerse food in a water bath whose temperature you control carefully. It can be hard to squeeze out all the air, so the bags tend to float and heat unevenly unless you weigh them down. Sous-vide cooking generally involves water temperatures between 120°F-180°F (49°C-82°C), which the heavy-duty bags can take."

Nathan Myhrvold, author of Modernist Cuisine also advised users to:

> "Avoid bags containing polyvinyl chloride (PVC). Ziploc bags for home cooks are a safe alternative because they are made from polyethylene (PE), which does not break down at the low temperatures of sous-vide cooking and are BPA-free."

A VERY SPECIAL *Thanks* TO OUR BACKERS

This book and our work on Codlo is made possible through the amazing support of our Kickstarter backers. Without them, you wouldn't be reading this today. Here's to each and every one of them!

135813	Aline Tran Hawaii 808	B & S Maddox	Brian Bell	Chris Bartlett
@londonned	Alkis	BA & EN	Brian Conner	Chris Dickey
@RichardSJust	Alvan Tom	badrobot	Brian Curtis	Chris Hockey
@Sillium	Amirul Khalid	Balazs Hollos	Brian Dahlem	Chris Khoo
@SparkDustJoe	Ammar H	Balu	Brian Davis	Chris Koo
0ng0	anders	Ban Xiong Tan	Brian Gerdes	Chris Leigh
3born	Anders Oedlund	Baron Von Oldenburg	Brian Hepler	Chris Little
A.	Andreas Eriksen	Barry O'Driscoll	Brian Hoffmeyer	Chris Perham
A. Del.	Andreas W	Bastien Kirsch	Britney Dupee	Chris Silivestru
A. Powler	Andrew Baglin	Beau Danger Reynolds	Bruce Marshall	Chris Simpson
A. Waning	Andrew C Rausch	Ben	Bryan	Chris Waiting
a.lber.to	Andrew Cook	Ben Abecassis	Bryon Shay	Chris Washburn
Aaron Ball	Andrew Do	Ben Cortez	Bryony	Christian Johansen
Aaron Bretveld	andrew dunn	Ben Craig	BWAT	Christian Morato
Aaron Carter	Andrew Head	Ben Decherd	C. Tyler Boyd	Christoph
aarphacker	Andrew Lee	Ben Edwards	Cameron F. McCord	Christophe Guéret
ackno	Andrew Mackenzie	Ben Eick	Cameron Jaccard	Christopher Cook
Adam Block	Andrew Prince	Ben Fan	Candra M.	Christopher Currie
Adam Dickinson	Andrew Shaffer	Ben Galang Jr.	Carl Downing	Christopher Jones
Adam F	Andrew Strout	ben lorente	Carmen Rooke	Christopher Lim
Adam Geller	Andrew Teoh	Ben Ross	Carol T Hutchinson	Christopher Munn
Adam Hill	Andrew Yardley	Ben T	Caroline Lee	Christopher Plowman
Adam Laskowski	Andy Shapiro	Benedict Teo	Carts	Christopher Salazar
Adam Murray	Andy Yuen	Benjamin L Rushing	Caryn Lim	Christopher Tan
Adele Asuncion	Ange Kritsas	Benny Ang	cataphoresis	Chun Liang
Adrian Drake	Anne Stoye	Benson Chua	Celia Poehls	Chun Seng Yip
Adrian Jen	Anon	Betty Wong	Celine Thong	Chung Tze Hoong Leslie
Adrian PyRoS Tan	Anon Y Mouse	bg	Charlene G.	Chung Yi Lin
Adrian Randall	Anonymous	bgt	Charles	Cindy W
Ahmed Al-Suwaidi	Anonymous eater of food	Bill Welliver	Charles Hoffmeyer	CK Tseng
Ai Pheng Y.	Anthony Coltman	Billy Hallett	Charles Scott Hargis	Claus F.
aigarius	Anthony Gross	blee	Charlie Hudson	Cleve Gibbon
Al	Anthony Wong	Bobby Gumenick	Charlie Seaman	Clifford Chin
Aleksey Kliger	Anton Grobman	Boschetti Francesco	Charlotte Lawrence	Clinton Henry
Alex Lathbridge	Antti Kupila	Maria	Chee Lup Wan	codlo
Alex Mathew	April Edwards	Brad Hsu	Chef Dawn Knowlton	Cody Lerum
Alex Moss	Arne Martin Aurlien	brandon tario	Chef Tank	Colin Ng
Alex Nager	arran james shaw	Brandon Vessey	Chien Liq	Colonel Fubar
Alex Teo	Arthur Watson	Brecht De Mulder	Chin Lai	Conrad Lee
Alexander Hawson	Asgeir Storesund Nilsen	Brenda Pomerance	Chip Hallett	Corinna Foong
Alexander Horvath	Ashvina	Brenda Tan	Choo Yan Bing	Cory Theobald
Alexandre Matamoros	athmane meziani	Brent Elliott	Chow	Courtney Krishnamurthy
Altoe	Atley Joseph	Brett Beck	Chris Anderson	cprofito
Alexis Muhly	B	brian	Chris B	Craig "The Coder" Dunn

Craig Schertz
Craig Toth
cuan
cwcobb
d
D Joseph
D Meikle
D S
D sun
Dale
Dale S Allen
Damien Innes
Damon Urban
Dan Sheline
Dan Webster
Dana Ang
Daniel C
Daniel Chou
Daniel Crandall
Daniel Flood
daniel khoo
Daniel Miles
Daniel Schell
Daniel Soh
Daniel Tosh
Daniel Westermann-Clark
Danio
dany k
Darah
Darlene Lopez
Darrell Ottery
Darren
Darren Farr
DarrylY
Dave
David
David "Skutchie" Perlman
David & Sheryl Guillory
David Berquist
david brearley
David Brown
David Goodrum
David H
David Hunter
David Jacobs
David Jessop
David Kleiner
David Leamy
David Lim
David Liu Lau
David Luk
David Morrison
David O'Neill

David Pesta
David Rowley
David Seo
David Silvernail
David Weber
David Weinehall
David Yi
Davis Glasser
Dean Carson
deana
Deanna
Debbie Landeck
Demian Vonder Kuhlen
Dempsie Morrison
Denese Ashbaugh Vlosky
Dennis
Dennis Chan
Dennis Flax
Dennis Kalpedis
Derek Gosselin
Derek Lum
Derek S Nettles
Derrick Matheson
Deven
Dfriedlaender
Diana Yund
DixieLadyChef
dlee
Dobbins
Don Inmon
Don Q
Doofus65
Dr.Seth
Dragan Angelovski
Dragonbait
Driscoma
Duncan Sample
DWolvin
Earthling
Ed labrador
Ed O'Brien
Ed Schumacher
Eddi
Eden Lau
Edmund Foong
Edwin
Einar A:
el_drako
Elena Ramirez
Ellen Cassidy
Elliott Gomez
Emily
Emily Blum
Emma Loke

emma w
Eoin Quinlan
Eric Damon Walters
Eric Henley
Eric Hervol
Eric Neufeld
Eric Norberg
Eric Pohl
Eric Puleo
Eric Sigler
Eric Wong
Erica Day
Erick
Erick Kwak
Erik Jan
Erin Hogg
Eugene Kim
Eugene Koh
Eugene Lazutkin
Eugene Pyatigorsky
Eunice Loo
Evan Deutsch
Evan Jones
Evelyn L.
Evgeny Filatov
Exitialis
Fabian Teichmueller
Fei Leung
Fernando
Fernando de la Flor
Fernando Ducloux
filgeo
Filippo Moncelli
Finbarr FArragher
Flavio Jandorno
Florian Tischner
Foo Suan Wee
Frances mak
frankie
Franklyn Hu
Fried Meulders
Frode Lundgren
Gabe Chai
gacteon
Garett Page
Gary
Gary Hatch
Gavin Chan
Gavin Chung
Gavin Tan
Gedas Simkus
Geoff Cooper
Geoff Dannatt
Geoffrey Ong Choon Jin
George McKelvey

Giacomo Ghezzi
gilad rozenberg
Giordano Bruno
Contestabile
GK
Glenn Rogers
Godfrey Borges
goeres
Goh Morihara
Gonzalo Saloma
Grace Wilton
Graham
Graham Abell
Graham Edmonds
Graham Hattersley
Graham Robertson
Grant Leung
Grant Lindsay
Greg
Greg Norman
Greg Sheets
Greg Tom
Grumpy Sam
Guy Watson
H.zegwaard
Hakim Ron
Hamza Hoummady
Han Hsien Seah
Hannes Brandstätter
Hans Puijk
Harethh AlJaghbir
Harry
Harry Adraktas-Rentis
Harvey Summers
Heather Disco
Hector Silva
Heiki Courcy Sunne
Hein Stander
Henry Lau
Ho Ching
Holly Barstow
Hoon Hyung Cho
Howard Spector
Hui Huang Lee
Humphrey Ho
hwangste
HydeChiu
Hye Kyong Im
I Know My Name
I. Novak
Iain Shirley
Iamtheceo
Ian Gould
Ian Koh
Ian L

Ian Normile
Ian Shorrock
Ian Swartz
Ian Upton
Ignacio Berberana
Irene Liow
ironjack
Izwan Zailan
J Mandel
Jackson Fields
Jacky Tang
jacqueline lee
Jacquilynne
Jakamoto
James
James Bailey
james dellow
James Ferguson
James Goillau
james hobbs
James Hoffmann
James Howard
james jones
James Payne
James Snodgrass
James Strachan
James Vonderharr
jamie
Jamie Ambrosius
Jamie Nichols
Jamie Schork
Jan Bolmeson
Jan Mechtel
Jan Self
Janek Sarjas
Jared
Jared A. Embree
Jarrad Clark
Jarret M. Streiner
Jason
Jason Bethel
Jason Curry
Jason Drilon
Jason Gilbert
Jason Liang
Jason McGuinness
Jason S.
Jason Stonehouse
Jason Wong
Jassie
JD Tan
Jean Duffy
Jeff Centeno
Jeff Craig
Jeff S.

Jeffrey
Jeffrey Kwan
Jeffrey Siaw
Jeffrey Warnock
Jenice Tom
Jenn Ong
Jennie Brotherston
Jennifer Ah-Kin
Jennifer Grothaus
Jenny L T Slater
Jens Jensen
Jeonghoon Lee
Jeremy Foo
Jeremy Palmer
Jeremy Shaw
Jeremy Sullivan
Jeremy Weathers
jeroens
Jesse Green
Jessica the Awesome
Ji Nok Ho
Jia-Hong Tan
Jian Yi
Jim & Paula Kirk
Jim Hu
Jim Jesse
Jim Lewallen
Jimmy Hong
Jin-Ping Lim
Jiska Ford
JM Sende
jmauricio
jmonty
Joanne Chung
Joby Catto
Joe Duckhouse
Joe Pugliese
Joel Gore
Joey Wong
johan duramy
Johan Nordberg
Johan Sundström
Johann Tay
John (EBo) David
John Allen
John Casteele
John Drummond
John G.
John Griffiths
John Gurnett
John Ho Chi
John K
John Kuszewski
John L.
John Leong

John M. Martinez
john naimoli
John Pedersen
John Rector
John Schieferle Uhlenbrock
John Udberg
John Watson
John Westlund the Magnificent
Jon Harrison
Jon Hudson
Jon O'Brien
Jon Suik
Jonathan H. Liu
Jonathan Kurtzman
Jonathan Mason
Jonathan Morgan
Jonathan Willmer
Jonathan Wong
Jonny Carr
Josef Drasch
Joseph A Sosa
Joseph Nastasi
Joseph Trevino
Josh D
Josh MacDonald
Josh Worley
Joshua Peng
Ju & Kel
Julia Kenny
Julian
Julien Lapensée
Jullie Lim
Justin Barabad
Justin Bloom
Justin De Nooijer
Justin Lam
Justin Teo
Justin Wynn
Jyri Lehtinen
K. Kim
K. Trinh
Kai S.
Kamäl Boucetla
Kamal Kishore Verma
Karina Ali Noor
Karli Watson
Kasper Bitsch Lund
Kaz de Groot
Keith Law
Kelley Greenlaw
Kelvin Tong
Kelvin Yip
Ken

Ken Cowin
Ken Mencher
Ken Yee
Keng San
Kenji Adrian Takeuchi
Kenneth
Kenneth Chien
Kenneth Lock
Kenneth Melich
kenny
Kenny Powers
Keropokman
Kerry Utton
Kerry Xie
Kevin
Kevin Chen
Kevin Greehey
Kevin Huang
Kevin LaChapelle
Kevin Ng SiJie
Kevin Novick
Kevin Rank
Khoo Chung Hoe
Kieron Bissett
Kieron Rooney
Kim
Kim T. Whitlow
Kit Chow
Kjell Magne Fauske
Koh Kah Hoe
Koh Yong Chia
Kolin Juckins
Kristian Aasgård
Kristine Jimenez
Kuli Singh
Kushal Banerjee
KW Lau
Kyle Bunker
L.C.Toh
Lamson Nguyen
Langdon
Larry Kwan
Larry Norder
Lars Malmqvist
Laura Cuellar
Laurens Peeters
Lawrence
Lawrence Green
Lawrence Lim
Layzer
Leandro Garcia Soto
Leewelo - Obsidian Order Lorekeeper
Leo S
Leon M

Lester Luo
lex deelder
Liang-Chen Yeh
Lilian W
Lim Kuo Yang
Linda Nicol
Lion Shmookler
Lisa & Abe
Lisa Mazurek
Liz Staunton
Lok Chow
Lorelei Rost
Lorraine J.
LP Chan
Lucius Wilson
Lukas
Luke Anderson
Luke Boniface
Luke Hayward
luke pankau
lumik
M. Dunn
Maaatt
Madalena Barata
Madeleine Villanueva
Maike
Malcolm James Harnden
Manuel Dolderer
Marc
Marc Elman
Marc Lee
Marcio F
Marco Aguiar
Marek Les
Maria Gaffney
Mark Albanese
Mark AR Thompson
Mark Dalton
Mark Hudspith
Mark Li
Mark Micallef
Mark Walton
Marko Cosic
Marshall C
Martin
Martin Coxall
Martin Deas
Martin Glassborow
Mary & Marleaux Flournoy
Matt Conway
Matt L
Matt Leach
Matt M.

Matt Nelson
Matt Phillips
Matt Risby
Matt Strickler
Matt Stuttle
Matthew Isoda
Matthew Miller
Matthew Morettini
Matthew Roy
Maureen M. Kananen
Max Condon
Max Raun
Max Temkin
Maxi
Megan & Yau
Melissa Bravin
MF Tan
Michael Ahmels
Michael Appleton
Michael Arnold
Michael Blow
Michael Boon
Michael Brennan
Michael Davidson
Michael Francesconi
Michael Gartland
michael grove
Michael Harris
Michael J Miller
Michael Jacob
Michael Josem
Michael K.
Michael Knowles
Michael Niccolai
Michael Quinlan
Michael Ravenel
Michael Shim
Michael Stein
Michael Wells
Michael Yartsev
Michael Yeh
Michal Malusek
Michel Wolfstirn
Michelle Chow
Michelle Lim
Mikael Götesson
Mike Allen
Mike Charnock
Mike Harrington
Mike Harris
Mike Leung
Mike Roach
Mike Sellers
Mike Williams
Milan Tuma

Mirko Junge
Mitchell Grimes
Mo
mobilabredband
Moises Ortega
Moizy
mojo
mona stallard
Monish Grover
Mont Buckles
Mr Charles Dlaper
Mr S. Zegar
Mr. Goat
Ms Shimite Offor
Mun Loon
myCodlo
N. Tay
Nate Lesiuk
Nathan
Nathan Skone
Nawtcher
neal kohl
Neal Kranes
Neil Chue Hong
Neil Graham
Neil Johnson
Neil W
Nekozuki
nerdegutt
Neural Echo
NG WEI LING
Nicholas C Mason
Nicholas Chua
Nick
Nick Wavish
Nico
Nicole Goh
Nigel J
No Name
Noah Bacon
Oishinboy
Ole Bahlmann
Oliver B.
Omid
P Bridson
p s terry
P-Dawg
Pablo
Pamela Francis
Pan Zheng Tao
Paolo
Patrick Baker
Patrick W. Hervey
Paul
Paul Grandy

Paul Maddison
Paul Nelson
Paul R. Pival
Paul Rabin
Paul Stables
Paul Uy
Pauli
pcn
PENGDAV
Perry Ong
Pete Kinnaman
Peter
Peter Griffiths
Peter Ho
Peter O.
Peter Orlov
peter plashko
Peter Sky Bognar
Petr Indian Konecny
Petteri Ojutkangas
Philip Ivanier
Philip Kwong
Philipp Solay
Phillip Scott
Phillip Stewart
Phoebe Holland
Phong Luu
Phrig
Phua Cheng Wee
Pierre Lonewolf
Polish
premal patel
Quah Wui Seng
Quan
Rachel Tan
Rafael Lopes de Melo
Raiman Au
Rajesh Patel
Ralf van Dooren
Ranjan Mitra
Raphael Javier
rasto subert
raszi
Raymond Fong
Raymond Lau
Raymond Ng
rbn
Reg Cheramy -
Stormboard
Reginaldo Spenciere
Reimer Mellin
Remington Ong
Remo Cornali
Ren
Reynaldo Caluag

Richard "BUZZtheBar"
Liang
Richard Alter
Richard Conti
richard emperado
Richard J Ramazinski
Richard Kingsbury
Richard Stocks
Richard Vahrman
Rick and Toni Sloane
Rick Chlopan
Ricky Hoots
RiverRat T
Rob L
Rob van der Veer
Robert Chen
Robert Erlick
Robert Gustavsen
robert maddox
Robert Mais
Robert Martin
Robert McNeil
Robin Seunghwan Lee
Ronald S Woan
Ronald Verheyden
Ronny Lizardo
Rory Bennett
Rosely
ROSS GRESHAM
roux
RS NL
RTS
Ru Te Teow
Rupert Gregory
Russell Fujimoto
Ryan Ark
Ryan P. Lee
Ryan W
S Canter
Sabrina Ko
Sagar Dhanasekhar
Sairam Suresh
Sam Gardom
Sam L. Roth
Sam Leung
Sam Shafie
Sandra Lee
Sandra Loerzer
Sanjay
Santos Correia
Sasathorn Phaspinyo
sassy palate
Sayilgan
Sco
Scong

Scott Gartner
Sean
Sean Frawley
Sean R Aung
Serge Poldi
Sergey Paliy
Sergio Garcez
Sham Das
Shaw Yean Lim
Shawna Gould
Shayn Harkness
Shien Wei Ooi
Shirley Tidor
Shiwei Huang
ShuSheep
Simon
Simon 'Silver' Rogers
Simon J
Simon Matti
Simon S Tan, MD
Sin Yi
slick8086
Some dude
Sonia Klemperer-
Johnson
Srikant M.
srinivas polineni
StartUp Genesis
Steel
Steen
Stefan Winkler
Stefano Driussi
Stephen K. Chiu
Stephen McCluskey
Stephen McDermott
Stephen Richards
Stephen Thomas
Stephen Yu
Steve Avery
Steven
Steven Bateman
Steven Burgess
Steven Chen
Steven Fagg
Steven Jones
Steven Parker
Steven Tong
Stidmon
Stuart Cole
Stuart Shelton
Sue Dowling
Sue H
Sue Wen Chiao
Sulaiman Jaafar
Sultan Saleh Al-Salem

Sung Woo Choi
sunny bates
Susanne Kollberg
Svend Holst
SY Tan
Sylvia Samantha
Sylvia Sim
T Yap
T. Tilash
Tai Nguyen
TDM
Ted Gould
terence chan
Terence Ling
Teresa Ozoa
Teri C.
Terry Ghozali
Terry Wong
The Delgado-Allens
The NYC Lakers
The Sammyness
The Swede
The Takai Frank Family
Thomas
Thomas Cannon, Jr.
Thomas Evans
Thomas Fitzgerald
Thomas Hedberg Jensen
Tiberius (or
TiberiusTeng)
Tim "Aardvark" Meakins
Tim Dutton
Tim Fleming
Tim Johnstone
Tim Nobes
Tim V.
Tim Wright
Timothée Revil
Ting Louie
TJ Ng
TM Chan
Todd 'Squirrel' Squire
Todd DeWitt
Tom Daniels
Tom Garrett
Tom Murton
Tom Viscelli
Tom Wilkinson
TOM WILLIAMS
Tom Young
Tommy Taknaes
Tony Cannon
Tony Kelly
Tony S
Tor Steinar Nilsen

ToToCraCra	Viet-Jamal Le	Wei	Wong Fook Fei	Yen Siow	Zhi Wei Kng
Trevin C.	Vincent GERMAIN	Wei Jie Loh	Wouter Schreuders	Yeo Puay Khoon	
Trey Williams	Vincent Tan	Wei Kiat	Wulf Forrester-	Yeong Yee	
trumpetó	vispillo	Wei Phin Tan	Barker	Troy Smart	
Tucker Snedeker	Vládíček Nováček	Wes Roe	WY	Errico Stigliano	
Tuomas Tolvanen	Wai Kin Wong	whittnee lachapelle	Xiaoping Li	Rhonda Weins	
Twyla G	Walter Wehner	Willard Korfhage	Xishan	Yi Chung	
U. Steurer	Wan Kong	William Gillett	Y. Chung	Yna Zuniga	
Vanessa Toh	Wandy Moo	William Ho	Yaniv Talmor	YNL	
Verloren	Warren Todd	William Otte	Yao Wei	Yu-Foong	
VHo	Warren Turner	William R	Yaocheng Lee	Yuting Lee	
Vicki Hsu	Wayne Conrad	William Sim	Yau Chung Ng	Yves Bastide	
Vicky Chan	Wayne Kwok	William Weissbaum	Yazz D. Atlas	Zach Kondo	
Victor Leong	Wee Kiat Teoh	Wolf Noble	Yee Yen	Zach Splaingard	

YOU'RE ALL *Awesome!*

Made in the USA
Lexington, KY
22 November 2014